PENGUIN BUSINESS

IMPACTFUL COMMUNICATION

Deepa Sethi is the dean, programmes and international relations, and professor, business communication, in the area of humanities and liberal arts in management at the Indian Institute of Management Kozhikode, India. With more than fifteen years of teaching and research experience, she specializes in business communication, soft skills, social media communication, advanced corporate communication and cross-cultural communication, among other areas. She has been published in and has guest-edited major academic journals. Experiential and activity-based teaching have been her forte, and she is known for her style of teaching, which has practical implications in addition to the theoretical underpinnings. Her training programmes on topics such as managerial effectiveness lab, communication effectiveness lab and soft skills for interpersonal effectiveness for working executives are highly acclaimed. Her faculty development programme, titled 'Innovative Approaches in Management Teaching', is much sought after.

Celebrating 35 Years of
Penguin Random House India

PRAISE FOR THE BOOK

'It's an excellent and very practical book on communication to build long-term relationships. I really enjoyed chapters on connecting cultures and learning to become an active listener'—Professor Jagdish N. Sheth, Charles H. Kellstadt Professor of Business, Goizueta Business School, Emory University, Atlanta, GA, USA

'*Impactful Communication: Communicate to Conquer* by Deepa Sethi is inspiring and enlightening. It is appealing and keeps you engrossed till the end!'—Sanjeev Bikhchandani, founder and executive vice-chairman, Info Edge (naukri.com, shiksha.com, naukrigulf.com, 99acres.com, jeevansathi.com)

'This is a must-read for all, just as Norman Lewis's *Word Power Made Easy* was when we were growing up, as much for those who possess great communication skills as for those who desire to. Great leaders, mind you, are all exceptional communicators. While some are gifted, most of them have had to work hard to become one. Look no further than *Impactful Communication: Communicate to Conquer* if you want to communicate like them and conquer like them. It is the most comprehensive yet lucid guidebook on communication and so aptly titled. Full credit to Professor Deepa Sethi for bringing it out at a time that's brought to the fore the importance of communication like never before. Read it, refer it, make it your constant companion and make the most of it!'—Neeraj Jha, group president and chief communications officer, The Bajaj Group

'Good communication skills are one of the most important human traits to have in the twenty-first century. Deepa Sethi's book *Impactful Communication: Communicate to Conquer* takes you down that path—a must-read!'—Parvin Dabas, actor, director and owner, Pro Panja League, Swen Entertainment Pvt. Ltd

'Deepa Sethi has authored a must-read for anyone considering understanding the nuances of communication. Read it and learn from one of the best!'—Salman Khan, senior manager, personnel, Oil India Limited

'*Impactful Communication: Communicate to Conquer* offers the most practical insights into communication, enumerating the real-world hands-on experiences which are the most important elements for professional success! This book by Deepa Sethi is indeed a road map to impactful communication'—K. Gnani Venkateswara Rao, additional general manager, HRD, ITI Ltd

Impactful
Communication

Communicate
to Conquer

Deepa Sethi

Series Editor: Debashis Chatterjee

**PENGUIN
BUSINESS**

An imprint of Penguin Random House

PENGUIN BUSINESS

USA | Canada | UK | Ireland | Australia
New Zealand | India | South Africa | China | Singapore

Penguin Business is part of the Penguin Random House group of companies
whose addresses can be found at global.penguinrandomhouse.com

Published by Penguin Random House India Pvt. Ltd
4th Floor, Capital Tower 1, MG Road,
Gurugram 122 002, Haryana, India

First published by SAGE Publications in 2021
Published in Penguin Business by Penguin Random House India 2023

10 9 8 7 6 5 4 3 2 1

ISBN 9780143463580

Typeset in Sabon by Manipal Technologies Limited, Manipal

www.penguin.co.in

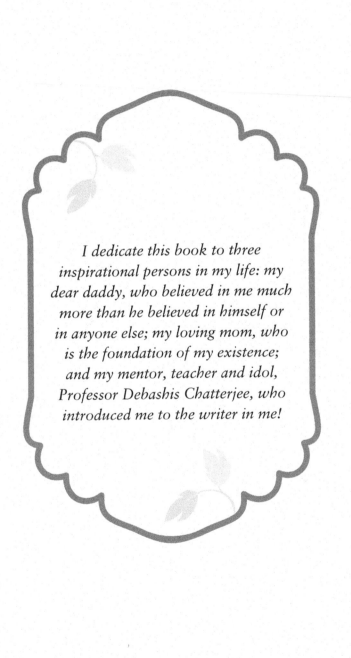

I dedicate this book to three inspirational persons in my life: my dear daddy, who believed in me much more than he believed in himself or in anyone else; my loving mom, who is the foundation of my existence; and my mentor, teacher and idol, Professor Debashis Chatterjee, who introduced me to the writer in me!

Contents

Note by Series Editor

Dear reader,

Penguin IIM Kozhikode (IIMK) Series for New Managers presents *Impactful Communication: Communicate to Conquer* from the esteemed faculty member of IIMK, Dr Deepa Sethi. The book is based on the author's first-hand experience in the field of communication, featuring unique tools to sharpen one's communication skills for the highly competitive corporate world.

The book begins with discussing the art of communication and its importance in the VUCA (volatility, uncertainty, complexity and ambiguity) world. The barriers to communication are evaluated with the help of seven vital Cs of communication. The book holistically takes on the varied aspects of communication such as listening, speaking, writing and body language. It explains how non-listening behaviours affect communication adversely and how these can be used constructively in exceptional situations to leave an indelible impression on the listener. This resource further discusses the role of verbal and non-verbal communication at the workplace, emphasizing the right choice of words and tone in communication.

Presentations in different formats are vital to business. Use of storytelling in presentation skills is another key feature of the book. It offers practical details on succinct handling of writing dexterity and covers the essentials of writing (creative writing, business writing and writing for the social media). The book also discusses the judicious use of claims–reason–evidence (CRE) framework of logical and persuasive writing in addition to logos, pathos and ethos suggested by Aristotle to make the content more structured and more meaningful.

While on the one hand the book ensures sensitization on the evolving nature of communication, on the other hand, it handles the issues of communication in the modern world of artificial intelligence (AI) and social media. The challenges of communication in the era of AI are debated, and insights into maintaining the personal touch of communication in a highly non-personalized world are advised. The use of effective communication on social media handles is another attribute of this book, where it effectively elaborates on the use of right hashtags, right words and right tone to win more attention and drive more traffic to specific social media handles. The four mantras for impactful communication in the book will also enlighten the readers in terms of valuing and reorienting themselves.

Impactful Communication and the other books in the Penguin IIM Kozhikode Series for New Managers aim to bridge the gap between the demands of the corporate world and quality of management education. As a new manager and professional, you will be ready to face the corporate world with greater clarity and confidence after reading the books in this series.

Debashis Chatterjee
Director
IIM Kozhikode

Preface

It all started when, one fine afternoon, I returned to my office after a class and received a message that the director, IIMK, Professor Debashis Chatterjee, had recommended that I work on this title. This proposal came at a point when I was seriously contemplating writing a book based on my teaching and research experiences, a book that would be a handy tool for everyone to possess, whether a young mind graduating from an institute or someone mature who was already working. Right intentions met timely intervention! That's how I delved into the writing of this book. Throughout the process, I have communicated with myself and had a dialogue with myself, and that has resulted in this book!

I began by jotting down the major topics I would want in the book and then proceeded with a broad outline for each. Thereafter, I nurtured every topic with care and love, adding empathy while writing. My experiences and interactions with the students in the classroom and outside, the moments of learning from my colleagues, the intriguing discussions with the director and the jiffies of enlightenment while having small talk with friends—I churned all these into this book.

When I read the book in the shape it has taken now, I am happily surprised. I realize that when the author pours out one's heart in writing, adding a lot of passion and a pinch of creativity to a text, the result is really authentic and satisfying. I hope you find the book interesting!

1

Communicating in the VUCA World

Uncertainty is an uncomfortable position. But certainty is an absurd one.

—Voltaire

We rarely get the chance to select certainty. Our lives have become quite exciting: we are interacting with Alexa and Siri, robots are doing our work, and IoT (the Internet of Things) has become a household name. Gone are the days of workplaces that were termed 'secure'. VUCA stands for volatile, uncertain, complex, and ambiguous, and is the 'new normal' in our organizations now. The digital epoch greatly influences the behaviour of everyone around us. What we need in this VUCA world is a paradigm shift with regard to building relationships at the workplace. No doubt, technology facilitates us in innumerable ways; however, it has reduced the number of real conversations we have with people. We communicate more through telephone, email, and social media than face-to-face. The human touch in our communication is lost somewhere. It should be remembered that the bonds we are able to develop in the present will determine the future of our organization. There is, thus, a dire need to transform our communication from a monologue to a dialogue and adopt empathy and compassion to develop and strengthen bonds that endure for a lifetime.

Imagine that your coworkers send you an email to congratulate you on being named 'best employee of the year'.

How much impact does it have on your boss when you request and present your case for a promotion through email?

Consider how it would affect the morale of employees who are informed of 'no incentive this month' due to a crisis by email versus face to face by an individual, a human being in person.

No technology can do what a human can: look into the eyes, empathize, sympathize and understand. Focus on human face-to-face communication more than through emails, message apps, chatbots, the phone, etc. Having said this, we cannot deny the advancement of technology and our dependence on it. The best option is to communicate effectively even while using technology.

But first, let us go to the basics of communication and explore how we can equip ourselves to embrace uncertainty, which is a fundamental trait of the VUCA world.

Scene 1
A to B: Please stand up.
B stands up.
A to B: You may sit now.
B sits down.

Scene 2
C to D: Which country do you belong to?
D: Denmark.

In Scene 1, A requested that B first stand and then sit, and B followed the request and instruction by first standing and then sitting down.

In Scene 2, C wanted to know which country D belonged to, and D told it.

Did A and C communicate in these two scenarios? Yes, they did. In simple terms, communication is to get the desired outcome. In the first scenario, the desired outcome for A was B's action of standing up and sitting down, which happened, while in the second scenario, the desired outcome for C was to know which country D belonged to, and she got to know it from D.

The word 'communication' draws its origin from the Latin word 'communicate', which means 'to share'. One of its definitions in the *Merriam-Webster* dictionary states, '[Communication is] a process by which information is exchanged between individuals through a common system of symbols, signs, or behavior.'

Communication is at the core of human and organizational existence. The process involves a sender who encodes a message, a medium through which the message is sent, and a receiver who decodes the message and gives feedback either through words—spoken or written—or through actions or non-verbally. This completes the cycle of communication.

Recipe to become an Effective Communicator

- 40 percent of an active listener
- 20 percent of an efficient presenter
- 20 percent of a quick thinker
- 20 percent of a win-win negotiator

The first ingredient in making an effective communicator is to be an active listener. One who listens well understands well, and one who understands well speaks well. Listening gives you the perspective and point of reference you need in order to communicate.

The second ingredient is to be an efficient presenter. Presentation does not only mean standing before an audience and speaking. It also means the grace, poise and dignity with which you carry yourself and behave, even when you are interacting with one person in your workspace.

The third ingredient is to be a quick thinker. In order to be a quick thinker, you need to be updated on the happenings around you, in your organization, in your state and country, and in the world. These updates facilitate your input during a discussion.

The fourth ingredient is to be a win-win negotiator. This happens when you empathize with the listener while speaking. When your efforts are towards communicating what you intend without causing harm to the other person's self-esteem while maintaining yours, it is called a win-win negotiation in communication.

Barriers to Communication

Due to the noise at different levels, communication often breaks down or gets messed up in the cycle above. This noise is termed 'barriers to effective communication'.

Let's look at some of the barriers.

Physical/Environmental Barriers

You are negotiating a deal with a client. All of a sudden, there's a power cut, which hampers your discussion for a few seconds. That is a physical barrier. On another occasion, you are discussing an important deal with the supplier in a restaurant, and a waiter interrupts, which is again a physical barrier. Physical barriers are quickly spotted and include closed doors, walls, noise (traffic, telephone ringing, machines, etc.), too hot or too cold room temperature, distance, time zones, dim lighting, unhygienic conditions, uncomfortable seats, etc.

Tip: Have open-concept workspaces. Choose face-to-face communication for sensitive communication. While writing, choose the right words and stay away from vagueness. Don't panic! Stay calm! Maintaining a calm attitude will facilitate focusing on the solution rather than the problem (barrier). Remember where you were interrupted and resume. While you take a pause to overcome the physical barrier, keep your receiver busy in discussion.

Physiological Barriers

You are at the suburban tram station in Paris and a little confused about which tram to take to reach your hotel. You ask the lady sitting on a bench. When she sees you speaking, she indicates with her actions that she is hearing impaired and also unable to speak. This is a physiological barrier. Other such barriers are vision impairment, speech disorders, poor listening skills, height, and other disorders related to the human mind and body.

Tip: Understand the reality, keep practical expectations, and try to figure out alternate ways of communicating. Remember, your intention is to have the receiver comprehend what you say and not have a different perception.

Psychological Barriers

You didn't get a pay raise, and now you're going to see a mentor for help. No matter how genuine she might be in giving advice, it is very evident that you are preoccupied with the pay raise refusal. This is a psychological barrier to effective communication, since you fail to listen to her advice and focus only on what has happened to you. Preconceived notions, emotions, prejudice, ego, attitude, opinions, inferiority complexes, stereotyping, biases, etc., constitute psychological barriers.

Tip: Have an open mind. Be aware of your state of mind and choose to be non-prejudiced while communicating. Consistently try to get over your emotions.

Social Barriers

Society has its own dynamics in terms of behaviour and norms. You are brought up in a family with a modern perspective on life based on equality. Let's say you are a female employee who joined a public-sector undertaking and have to report to your male supervisor. On your first day, you say hello to him and find that he is taken aback. Now he talks to you with an intimidating frown whenever you meet him. This is a social barrier to effective communication since different upbringings based on social norms related to gender have created issues. Values, age, socio-economic status, and marital status are other social barriers.

Tip: Learn to have an open mind towards others. Even if you are perceived differently by your receiver, there is no reason for you to get anxious or intimidated in their presence. Behave normally and ensure that you keep on building your credibility through your workplace etiquette, work ethics and behaviour.

Language and Semantic Barriers Are Not Cool!

Similar words and symbols differ in meaning. Semantics is the study of the meaning of words and symbols. Semantic barriers arise when the receiver's interpretation of the message differs from what the sender intended. These arise in the encoding and decoding parts of a message.

> A, on seeing gulab jamuns on the table, calls the serving staff.
>
> A: Are these gulab jamuns hot?
>
> Serving staff: No, sir, these are sweet.

After moving from there, both A and the serving staff have their fill of laughter at each other's expense. Did you get it?

The denotation and connotation of the word 'hot' caused all this confusion and amusement. The word 'hot' is associated with being spicy in some parts of our country; so, when A asked whether the gulab jamuns were hot (he meant temperature), the serving staff uttered that those were sweet. A was amused at the behaviour of the serving staff, thinking he was out of his mind to confuse temperature with taste, while the serving staff was in peals of laughter, thinking how a dessert could be 'hot' (spicy). This is an example of a semantic barrier. Other semantic barriers include regional influence, poor pronunciation, poor expression, faulty translation, slang, jargons, etc.

Now, let's consider another instance. On your last visit to Spain on a company assignment, you were baffled when you landed at the airport and saw that there was no one to drop you off at your hotel. There were placards around written in Spanish. When you wished to seek clarification, the local drivers spoke Spanish. Without an iota of the language, you felt really lost. This is an example of a language barrier. For communication to be effective, you ought to have learned the basics of the language of the country or state you are visiting.

Tip: Be very specific in your choice of words to overcome the semantic barrier. Avoid vague expressions such as probably, right away, usually, you know, and always, as well as jargon. Instead, use words that have a single meaning to be clear in your communication. Overcome language barriers by using actions to describe what you wish to convey; however, if you need to live in a society with a foreign language for a long time, learn at least the basics of the language.

Technological Barriers

Technology has made things a lot easier and more convenient for us. However, it comes with its own challenges.

> A speaking to B over a Zoom meeting.
> A: Let's finalize the project report today.
> B: Definitely. Please initiate the presentation.
> A shares the screen, the slideshow starts and A, simultaneously, explains how they should proceed. And oops!
> B: I am sorry, your voice is breaking. I did not get the last part of your sentence.

So, this is one example of a technological barrier. Other such barriers include call drops due to network issues, a misunderstanding of emojis and symbols, microphone failure, computer or laptop breakdown, corrupt software, and so on.

Tip: Don't let technology replace or rule you. Always have a backup plan. Even if a technological barrier is created, remain patient until the problem is solved; if it persists, continue with your communication as if nothing had happened. Consider it a minor issue and carry on.

Cultural Barriers

You remember the lady on the bench in the example for the physiological barrier. Like you, someone else also wants to know something about her. She says through her actions that she understands people by reading their lips. This other person is wearing a veil on her face, due to which only her eyes are visible. The lady cannot see the lips of this person. This is an instance of a cross-cultural barrier to effective communication, where the veil is mandatory in public places in a particular culture, due to which the lady is unable to read the lips.

Cultural barriers are the first fruits of globalization. The variety in cultures, whether national or organizational, may cause barriers if there is a clash. Cultural barriers include mannerisms, the display of emotions, non-verbal behaviour such as winking of the eyes, gestures, stereotyping, traditions, and religion.

Tip: Begin by accepting that you are two different people. This will facilitate your staying away from stereotyping. Make use of a mutually understandable medium of communication and avoid encroaching on the private space of the receiver. Be open to learning from new cultures. Find common ground to work together. Help your receiver comprehend what you mean. Accommodate cultural differences by being sensitive to and aware of the cultural differences that exist around you, and, finally, learn about new cultures.

Organizational Barriers

Most managers believe that their team is good for nothing. These are barriers related to hierarchy and status in an organization and are termed as organizational barriers.

Scene 1

Two managers, while having tea:

M1: My team doesn't do anything. I am always anxious about timelines because of these people.

M2: I agree. If I don't push and nudge, I am sure no one will complete work on time.

Scene 2

Two colleagues talking during lunch time in the canteen:

D: Finally, I am meeting the boss today at 3 pm. I had asked for his appointment last week.

E: Even I wanted to see her to discuss an important thing. Will call her secretary to seek an appointment for tomorrow.

Here, we see that protocols need to be followed before meeting the boss. This is an organizational barrier. Other such barriers include information overload, ambiguous planning, structure, and rules and regulations.

Tip: Do a background search on the organization before you join to ensure a smooth adjustment once you do join. Learn by observing the behaviour of your colleagues and the process of communication with internal and external stakeholders, both written and oral, and adapt to the organizational culture. Organizational culture is largely a product of power distance (PD) in societies; however, keep in mind that even in the same societies, there might be organizations with different cultures.

Avoid Communication Shutdowns

There are certain statements that place the listener in an awkward situation, cause embarrassment or offence, and stop the flow of communication. Keep away from these statements, often termed 'communication shutdowns'.

- Don't be ridiculous.
- We've never done that before.
- We will become the laughing stock of the entire company.
- Let's form a committee to . . .
- Let's get back to reality.
- It's not in our budget.

- It won't work here.
- I don't personally agree, but if you insist . . .

Seven Cs of Communication

1. **Completeness:** This refers to furnishing complete information while communicating. Incomplete information very often leads to confusion, misunderstanding, or miscommunication since the receiver is left to complete the information, which is generally subjective.

The balance due is on page 1 of this document. (Incomplete)
The balance due is on Page 4 of this document. (Complete)

2. **Correctness:** This refers to being correct in whatever you communicate. Incorrectness may be the result of ignorance about some information or of misrepresenting information intentionally or unintentionally. Whatever the reason, incorrectness in communication may be perceived as dishonesty and a lack of ethics.

The Constitution of India came into effect on January 26, 1947. (Incorrect)
The Constitution of India came into effect on January 26, 1950. (Correct)

3. **Conciseness:** This implies being to the point and brief while communicating. Instead of beating around the bush, try to communicate as concisely as possible.

We wish to inform you that our company is very happy with the belief you have shown in us. (Wordy)
   We value your beliefs. (Concise)

4. **Concreteness:** This is the opposite of abstractness or vagueness. Vagueness in communication leads to misperception in the absence of vivid imagery. Use verbs that indicate concrete pictures rather than abstract, blurry images.

ABD Pvt. Ltd made huge profits this financial year as compared to the last. (Vague)
   ABD Pvt. Ltd made 15 per cent more profits this financial year compared to the last. (Concrete)

5. **Clarity:** Be absolutely clear while communicating. While communicating, your objective is to get the desired outcome by communicating at the level of the receiver. The outcome cannot be achieved if you communicate in order to display your vocabulary and knowledge. Use words that are easily understood and cannot be misinterpreted.

The report was about executives suppressed by age and gender. (Unclear)

The report focused on the age and gender of executives. (Clear)

6. **Courtesy:** This intends to be courteous while communicating. However, it does not require you to overdo courtesy.

Their standards are fixed: He has to be a researcher and a good instructor. (Discriminatory)
Their criteria suggest that he or she should be a good researcher and a good instructor. (Courteous)

7. **Consideration:** It is also referred to as the 'first-you attitude' and suggests giving more importance to your receiver by being receiver-centric. Communicate in a manner in which your receiver perceives what's in it for them rather than trying to locate some hazy objective behind your communication.

We're happy to let you know that we're going to be open longer to make shopping easier. (I-centric/egoist)
You will be able to shop late into the evening with the prolonged working times. (Considerate)
You did not attach your demand draft to the envelope. (Insensitive)
The envelope we received did not have a demand draft in it. (Considerate)

How to Handle Communication in a VUCA World?

Now that the seven Cs of communication are clear, let's polish the way we communicate in today's VUCA world (e.g., Twitter).

Keep It Simple

Cut the clutter! Forget long texts, emails, and videos! Experiment with the limited characters' availability on Twitter! Use the right characters to make your communication simple and hit the bull's eye!

Let's appreciate Jeff Bezos's concise and catchy tweet: Jeff Bezos, @JeffBezos

Hey, India. We're rolling out our new fleet of electric delivery rickshaws. Fully electric. Zero carbon. #ClimatePledge

Reinforce

Reinforce your message using various methods because Twitter alone is not enough. People retain appealing messages in varied forms. Come up with ground-breaking ideas. Create videos, use different social media platforms, and podcast. Go beyond the regular to be impactful!

Another example to learn from:
ASPCA@ASPCA

Animal cruelty happens all year long; don't take a vacation from helping animals this summer. Pls RT & donate today: bddy.me/2f8XOHz

Plan and Strategize

Build stories and narratives around themes, use props to tell them, keep them in order, and keep your audience interested in the content and the way you tell it!

Strike a Chord

Engage in a conversation with people. Whether it's a colleague or a client, meaningful exchanges go a long way in building relationships. Develop a dialogue; don't limit yourself to a monologue! Let people ask you questions, let them give you suggestions, and, above all, let them be themselves.

Remember, whether you are branding your organization or yourself, you need a brand communication strategy, and such a strategy is best when it is digital!

The Brand Named 'You'!

In the hunky-dory city of Joy, there is a person named Smile. Everyone enjoys Smile, and Smile is grateful for everyone. Smile has the most friends of all because Smile knows the art of making everyone happy!

You have the utmost responsibility of creating and nurturing the brand called 'you'. There are various ways in which you can develop a network for this brand. Speed networking is one such way in which you highlight this brand.

Speed Networking

Unlike traditional networking events—which gather specific groups of people, such as small business owners and job seekers, at a particular time and place, and the groups have to form connections on their own—speed networking is a way forward because the event is structured in a manner that enables every person at the venue to speak to everyone present there.

Speed networking denotes a business meeting. It aims to speed up the creation of business networks. It is a process where members meet for interaction and knowledge sharing. They have brief exchanges with each other with regard to their work backgrounds and career goals.

Speed networking facilitates the broadening of networks for better opportunities and collaborations. This concept is gaining popularity these days due to its format, which allows you to expand your network systematically in a short span of time.

It caters to many different interests and can help you get the experience you need in the fields you choose.

I strongly believe in speed networking. It enables me to break the ice and interact with a number of people and facilitates my longer conversations with them later on. It also lets me understand how I am explaining my new venture. In one speed networking session, I tell my story at least 10 times and gain mastery over it with the help of immediate feedback.

Formats of Speed Networking

Round Robin

This is a common format where one group rotates and interacts with one individual every few minutes. In such a format, every attendee is able to interact with 7–8 people in sixty minutes.

Group

In this format, some people are assigned to a group where they get introduced to each other and interact for about ten minutes. The organizers decide on the criteria before grouping.

Station

This format is a bit unique. All participants need to fill out a questionnaire before the event, mentioning their current profile and who they would be interested in interacting with. These will then be numbered and allotted to stations with similar fits, where they are required to spend a particular amount of time.

Excelling at Speed Networking

Prepare

The first and foremost thing you need to understand is the format of the event. Accordingly, you need to prepare for the event to make the best use of your time by forming meaningful networks. Choose the event judiciously. Very often, people consider it a networking meeting. Please understand the difference. You go to speed networking meetings with the intention of forming associations that will aid your prospects and future, not just create another bunch of acquaintances interested in keeping in touch for social reasons.

Speed networking has little or no space for small talk. Be ready with a focus on an interaction with an objective. Have clarity of thought regarding the message you wish to convey. This does not come easy for some, but practice helps. Carry your business cards, a description of your organization, your profile, a folder, and a decent pen.

Goal Orientation

Begin thinking backwards. Suppose you are looking for a new role in another industry, say the apparel industry; do some groundwork with regard to key profiles working in that industry and ensure you join the speed networking meetings with such attendees. Even if you don't come across such people immediately, there is a possibility they might introduce you to such individuals. Carefully retain the business cards they share and study these after every speed networking session.

Be Authentic

Remember the basic rules of politeness while meeting people. The 'speed' factor is so fascinating that, at times, politeness is compromised to achieve it. Share the required courtesies. Exchange business cards and wait for the other person to initiate the conversation. Introduce yourself if the person doesn't initiate. Ensure that along with your contact details, your business card includes your LinkedIn profile, another professional network's details, and your website with your professional background.

By waiting for the other person to start, you are showing that you are a good listener. This also helps you learn about the person's interests, so you can move the conversation forward by finding something you both like. This is what makes speed networking work. Be authentic and smart while introducing yourself.

Cherishing the First-You Attitude

A first-you attitude is, most of the time, a win-win strategy in speed networking. Don't be anxious over running out of time; be patient. By allowing the person to speak, you are giving your time and attention and, in the process, gaining a sense of network and understanding. Without much effort, the first-you attitude paves the way for mutual benefit where reciprocation is the key element and both gain in the process.

Be Mindful of the Brand Called 'You'

Be clear about your goals and aspirations, along with the motivation behind everything. Have clear expectations from speed networking. Be dressed in the attire expected at the event. Be aware of your strengths and prepare to articulate them succinctly. Make the best use of your body language and paralanguage during the event. Assess through body language what the other person thinks about you while you are in a conversation.

Keep Your Elevator Pitch Ready!

A thirty-second byte about yourself is known as an 'elevator speech'. Being prepared with an elevator speech makes speed networking a cakewalk! Your pitch should consist of all that you would like to share. Rehearse and make it appear as effortless as possible. An effective thirty-second pitch will ensure you have receivers concentrating and focusing on everything you share after it. Take short breaks after a minute to listen so that you can weave what the receiver wants into your conversation and make it mutually beneficial.

Essentials of an Effective Elevator Pitch

- Your name, designation, and organization
- Your skills with real-time examples
- What makes you 'you'?
- Your aspirations
- Your expected outcome from the meeting

Have Speed Networking Questions Ready

- What do you do?
- What motivated you to come here today?
- What do you like the most about the work you are doing now?
- What are some skills that are imperative to succeeding in the work you are doing?
- Your career story is insightful. Could you please share more about your first job?
- Based on what I shared about myself, what kinds of roles would you suggest for my kind of profile?
- I appreciate the way you handled the challenges in life. What are those two things that you strongly stand for?
- How do you think I may help you transition to another industry?

- What do you suggest that I do to move ahead in my career?

Note-Taking

Note-taking during speed networking is very helpful and offers long-lasting benefits. Note the details of your interaction: who you are talking to, the date, the context, and a summary of the discussion. Note-taking creates a positive impression of you as being interested and alert.

Continue the Connection

Continue the connection even after the event. If you don't plan to follow up, it's better not to waste time on speed networking. Of course, don't overdo it and don't nag. A brief phone call or a short email facilitates a lasting impression and professionalism. Your notes will be helpful after a brief discussion over the phone or email.

Introspect

Think critically about every speed networking event you attend. Assess your behaviour, body language, and choice of words, and analyse what could have been done differently for better outcomes. Keep getting better!

Communicate as a Leader in the VUCA World

The VUCA world expects you to communicate like a leader. Why? Because a leader focuses on not only getting a job done well but also nurturing stronger relationships within the organization, if every person communicates like a leader, the synergies will together lead to a congenial work environment.

Follow these tips to communicate as a leader.

Keep It Simple

In the world of Twitter and Instagram, there is a need to craft short, crisp messages with substance. Keep it simple and to the point.

Your tweet about underpinning objectives may read as follows:

'Our new product, GAME, is at 70 percent of its goal; let's create further awareness.'

Reinforce Multiple Mediums Using Different Formats

Your message needs to be repeated often and in different ways, because a single tweet might not be enough and you need to keep it interesting. Experiment with techniques; create a podcast; do a web conference; there are unlimited options to be innovative.

Converse with People

The VUCA world expects you to converse with people, not talk at them. Go that extra mile and take that extra step to convert your statements into conversations. Make people around you comfortable enough to discuss things with you, share issues with you, and hopefully look at you, if not for a solution then at least as a good listener.

In a Nutshell

The long-term goal of communication is to build and nurture relationships. Whether these are face-to-face or virtual, whether these are within the organization or outside, whether you live in the VUCA world or not, it is most important to stay in touch through communication. Your network goes a long way towards shaping you as an employee, a colleague, a team leader, a team member, and an individual. Your efforts in creating and maintaining networks never go to waste!

2

All Ears

When you talk, you are only repeating what you know;
but when you listen, you may learn something new.

—Dalai Lama

Becoming a Better Communicator through Effective Listening

How many times has someone come to you with 'one' problem and left with 'many'? You are smiling! Yes, our biggest issue is not that we do not listen; it's the time we devote to speaking more than listening. Most of the time, we follow the 30:70 formula, where we listen 30 percent of the time in a conversation and speak 70 percent of the time.

You should already know that the most important thing you can do to improve your communication skills is to learn how to listen well. And that will happen once we reverse the formula and make it 70:30, where we listen 70 percent of the time and speak 30 percent.

Did you know that listening is a choice, an art, and a gift? It is a choice since it is with the mind and is conscious. It is an art because it can be developed. It is a gift since it encompasses ideas, attitudes, and emotions and involves your time spent in the process.

Listening is the ability to precisely receive and infer messages during the communication process. Listening leads to effective communication. In the absence of active listening, messages are certainly misinterpreted. The outcome is that communication snaps, which in turn upsets and annoys the sender of the message and strains relationships, whether personal or professional.

Listening and Hearing: Are They the Same?

Are you aware that your ears continue to hear even when you are sleeping? It's just that your brain is ignoring those sounds.

Listening	Hearing
You do not listen to every sound that falls on your ears. When you move leisurely in a garden, you enjoy listening to the chirping of the birds.	You hear every sound that falls on your ears. When you are playing with your friends in the garden, you are hearing the chirping of the birds.

Physical and mental process since it involves ears, head and heart. Your ears are engaged in catching the sound of birds chirping while your brain is enjoying the sound and sending signals to your heart to be involved in it.	Physical process since it involves ears to hear. Your ears are catching the sound of birds chirping along with other sounds around you.
Voluntary since it requires focus and effort both. You relate the soft chirping sound to your mental state.	Involuntary since it requires neither focus nor effort. The chirping sound has no effect whatsoever.
You have a choice to listen. You strain your ears and concentrate on the notes.	You have no choice to hear. Chirping sound is falling on your ears.
The said and the unsaid are listened. Your brain tries to identify the birds' purpose behind the chirping.	Only the said (sound) is heard. The chirping doesn't affect you.
Active process. You are enjoying it.	Passive process. You don't care about the chirping.

Now that we have established that listening is definitely not the same as hearing, let's explore how effective listening helps.

Rewards of Effective Listening

Understanding concepts and ideas in a better way and forming associations between them are the rewards of listening.

Professional Life	Personal Life
High self-esteem	Enhanced confidence
Leadership skill	Cordial family relationships
Synergy in teams	More friends
Customer satisfaction	Better grades
Higher productivity	Enriched health

Listening as a Process

We generally think that it takes the presence of an ear and the brain's sensing abilities to make listening happen. But did you know that birds have sonic listening powers but no ears? They only have holes on each side of their brains. Hence, it is not just about having big ears or using a bunch of words; listening is a whole process of sensing verbal and non-verbal cues.

Listening involves not just what is said but also how it is said. It is much more than listening to the words. Listening incorporates grasping both verbal and non-verbal messages. In fact, when you are able to sense the verbal and non-verbal messages with ease, you start your journey to becoming an effective listener. Listening is a cohesive process that comprises focus, comprehension, evaluation, empathy, and feedback. These form an integral part of the effective listening process and happen simultaneously in sync with each other.

1. **Focus:** The right frame of mind is a prerequisite for effective listening. This leads to a focus on what is being said (both verbally and non-verbally) and how it is said. Focus implies the absence of distraction. It requires complete concentration on what is being said, through words and without words, and not allowing any other idea to interfere with the dedicated attention. While maintaining focus, the listener needs to deliberately try to keep away from thoughts that get in the way of listening. You should focus on the words and also on the tone, pitch, and voice modulation, in addition to the body language, while listening.

2. **Comprehension:** While focus leads to total attention on the said and the unsaid, comprehension leads to interpreting the intended meaning. You need to fully comprehend the message received in order to be a part of the communication. Your listening should transform the message into a dialogue resulting in an interaction, whether you choose to speak or not. Your knowledge and experience colour your comprehension.

3. **Evaluation:** Focus and comprehension should further lead to the evaluation of the received

message. Your critical thinking ability is instrumental in the evaluation of the essence of the message. Your interest in the speaker and the message leads to a fruitful evaluation.

4. **Empathy:** Accepting that everyone has a perspective and a viewpoint facilitates having an open mind while listening. This is precisely the beginning of empathy in listening. You may agree or disagree with the speaker, but once you are open to viewpoints, you will let people speak their mind.

5. **Feedback:** Feedback happens when you assimilate what you heard with regard to your own experiences. Response may be in terms of a sound such as 'um' and 'ah', or word/s such as 'OK', 'I see', and 'fine', question/s such as 'is it?' and 'how?' or gestures such as head nods and eye movements.

Types of Listening

Most of the listening required in business can be categorized as follows:

Informative listening: The first day of starting a new job is a bag of excitement, apprehension, and confusion. While you are figuring out where to start, you are informed that you are supposed to attend a briefing with the heads of different departments. How keenly you would listen to each and every piece of information shared, noting down the important things and actively participating in the question-and-answer (Q&A) session to sort out your queries. This is informative listening. It is meant to gain information and requires complete attention. The purpose is to acquire correct and complete information. Details of the information are required to be stored for retention and future use. Other instances of informative listening are information sessions, briefing sessions, etc.

Active listening: In a client meeting, while negotiating a big deal for an ambitious project, you are engrossed wholeheartedly in the discussion, making every effort to address every issue raised by the other meeting attendees handling the minute details. This is active listening. It is the most ideal form of listening. Here, you deliberately concentrate on what the speaker is sharing. You do not let your attention break loose. This type of listening is complex and is ingrained with practice. It requires paying complete attention to the speaker and being perceived by the speaker as 'listening'. In the absence of the latter, the speaker may get the impression that you are not interested or disengaged with the speaker. The non-verbal cues to convey that you are actively listening are maintaining eye contact, giving head nods, using gestures, and smiling, while the verbal cues are using words like 'yes' or filler words such as 'oh, really?', 'uh-huh', 'hmm', and 'indeed'. Verbal cues also include asking questions and seeking clarification, paraphrasing, summarizing, and so on. This verbal and non-verbal 'feedback' not only encourages the speaker to communicate openly and easily but also augments the speaker's confidence in you. Other instances of active listening are business interactions, feedback sessions, interviews, meetings, etc.

Empathetic listening: When a client comes to you with a complaint, you would want to resolve it in order to maintain professional and cordial relations with the client. And any complaint that you can understand from the client's perspective enables you to solve it better. This is empathetic listening. It is a very powerful form of listening. In addition to the traits of an active listener, you need to make an effort to comprehend the emotional meaning of what has been said. In active listening, you respond verbally and/or non-verbally. In empathetic listening, you also try to feel both the speaker's content and context to figure out the underlying message. Examples of empathetic listening include customer relations, counseling sessions, some aspects of performance, and hiring and disciplinary interviews.

Passive listening—the communication killer: Passive listening is just a bit better than hearing. Nevertheless, it is ineffective since it is listening without responding or even reacting. Consequently, it may be seen as a monologue, where the speaker speaks but the listener does not register what is being said. Hence, it emerges as a communication killer because communication necessarily entails a dialogue, a two-way exchange.

Passive listening encompasses no answer in any form—verbal or non-verbal. Passive listeners act either responsively or unresponsively according to their temperament and attitude. Their minds strolled to related thoughts and descriptions. Passive listening instances would be listening to the news, listening to disengaging lectures, etc. When attention wanders during this form of listening, it's often not a problem. Passive listening is fine for many forms of enjoyment. This type of listening, however, would be inappropriate in face-to-face conversations and other business circumstances.

We indulge in this form of listening while doing multiple things at a time, like listening to the spouse while working on the laptop. When the spouse asks if you have watered the garden, you may respond 'yes' without actually meaning it. As long as you are listening passively at home, you can still manage to repair the damage. But if you are a passive listener at work—with your team members, clients or customers, managers or bosses—you might be in trouble. Remember, when you are listening to someone passively, you are showing disregard for them.

Barriers to Active Listening

Physiological: Physiological barriers may be due to hearing impairment of the listener or speech issues of the speaker. The non-fluency of the speaker may also become a hindrance to active listening.

Physical: External noises in the form of sounds in the environment are termed 'physical barriers', such as loud machine sounds, traffic noise, and frequent phone calls and messages. The varying temperature of the place where the communication is taking place is another physical barrier to active listening. Distance from the speaker also affects active listening.

Psychological: Preconceived notions, presumptions, prejudices, emotions, mental-cultural blocks, judgements, biases, and subjectivity comprise psychological barriers to active listening. For example, when you are angry while listening, you might misunderstand the speaker.

The EPG of Active Listening

Just like the ECG (electrocardiogram) shows how healthy your heart is, the EPG speaks a lot about how healthy (active) your listening is.

E stands for eye contact. Maintain eye contact to motivate the speaker. However, don't intimidate the speaker by staring. It is advisable to look at the person, not into their eyes.

P stands for posture. Posture is an indicator of your interest in the speaker. Don't lean backward. Instead, slightly lean forward while listening.

G stands for gesture. Gestures are very important while listening. Your head nod and minimal gestures show the speaker that you are listening keenly. Gestures go hand in hand with facial expressions while listening, such as facing the speaker, not crossing arms, and smiling. Avoid fidgeting while listening.

Let's take a look at a scenario now.

A to B: My manager said that I might get more incentives this month.

B to C: A, very happily, told me that she will get more incentives every month.

In this case, three significant problems occurred:

Addition of cues: Very happily told me . . .
Omission of cues: Manager said . . .
Distortion of cues: 'This' month has become 'every' month.

While it is vital to follow the EPG of active listening, equally important is refraining from actions that hinder the process. So, say a strict no-no to AOD (addition—omission—distortion).

> Boss: Why is Raj resigning?
> Supervisor: He has been frustrated for months.
> Boss: He should have told me.
> Supervisor: He tried doing so.

The above conversation sounds familiar, doesn't it? Bosses generally find it difficult to listen to bad news or negative messages and might be sending subtle signals that dissuade frank and open feedback. The implicit Power Distance in the so-called open organizations discourages people from speaking their mind. These are termed 'non-listening behaviours' because of the absence of effectiveness while listening.

Pseudo Listening

> Daughter sharing the day's activity with mother suddenly stops and looks at the mother.
> Daughter: Mom, are you here?
> Mom: Yes dear, go on.
> Daughter: That's fine.

Excellent eye contact, head nods at regular intervals, and hmms and ums while listening do not always prove one to be an active listener. In fact, it is termed 'pseudo listening', which means 'like listening', where eye contact is present, required gestures are there, and filler words are used, but the listening is passive. Hence, pseudo listening is a type of non-listening behaviour. Pseudo listeners are those who convey the impression of being alert. They smile, nod their heads, and even use words such as 'is it?' and 'oh, OK!' but actually they pay no heed to the speaker.

Defensive Listening

Ronnie delayed the submission of his project report. He explained how network issues at his workstation caused the delay. His manager, Jay, understood the situation, empathized with him, and accepted the late submission. Another fortnight passed. Jay convened a meeting of all the teams to discuss the details of a new project. While concluding the meeting, the following conversation took place:

> Jay: No excuses will be entertained in case of delays. Ensure timely submission.
> Ronnie: Boss, but I shared a genuine reason for my delayed submission.

Ronnie demonstrated 'defensive listening.' Jay was making a general statement with regard to another project, but Ronnie took it personally. Defensive listeners receive harmless remarks personally and consider these as personal criticisms. This type of behaviour portrays defensive listeners as insecure and low on confidence.

Selective Listening

> HR manager: This quarter, our organization has decided to give performance-based incentives as festival bonus in addition to the monthly salary.
>
> Employee (to herself): Wow, festival bonus! I will buy the laptop that I have been longing to buy.

This precisely is 'selective listening', where the employee took mental note of the festival bonus and conveniently overlooked the most important aspect of performance-based incentives as the festival bonus. When the listener chooses what to listen to, it is called 'selective listening'. Selective listeners tend to grasp only those slices of a message that they are interested in or that benefit them, conveniently discarding all other matters. They select what they want to listen to and are least interested in anyone else's views.

Insulated Listening

> Employee: I have an urgent work at home. May I leave early today?
>
> Manager: Yea, these urgent works just keep one busy! Please come to my office with the XYZ project file. I need some clarifications in the calculations. I will be meeting their team leader at 3 in the afternoon today.

Here, the manager chose 'what not to listen'. This is 'insulated listening'. The topic has not changed. However, it is not addressed either. Insulated listeners, as opposed to selective listeners, choose what not to listen. Insulated listeners evade and ignore specific themes or issues and are switched off when a particular issue crops up in a discussion.

Stage Hogging

Tara meets her colleague Meera in the office on Monday.

Tara: Hi, Meera. What did you do on the weekend?

Meera: Hello, Tara. This weekend, I went to the Blitz shopping mall to . . .

Tara: Oh, shopping! I love shopping. I too went to the Blitz shopping mall. What did you buy?

Meera: Winter is approaching, so I bought a cardigan for . . .

Tara: Yes, this time, the winter is going to be severe. I have already bought cardigans for all of us. Did you visit the recently inaugurated patisserie?

Meera: Yes, I . . .

Tara: The stuff they sell there is delicious. OK. Let's get to work now.

As the name indicates, this points out an attitude of being the centre of attention. Stage hogs are in love with their own voices. Their agenda is just to voice their opinions and share their ideas. They generally have no concern whatsoever with others' points of view on the topic. They always seem to be performing orations and delivering rapid talks and rarely listening.

Insensitive Listening

> Tim: Harry, I want to share something very personal urgently.
>
> Harry: OK, please say what you want to say quickly. I need to make an important call in two minutes.
>
> Tim: Oh! It's OK. You carry on.

Insensitive listening implies listening without sensitivity to what the speaker is saying. Insensitive listeners concentrate only on the apparent implication of the speaker's words. They are not able to listen beyond the face value of the other's words. They seldom understand the underlying sense of what is said. They also overlook elusive, non-verbal signals.

Ambushing

The term 'ambush' means to hide and attack suddenly. Ambushing is to listen to a person with the intent to attack and not to understand.

During a weekly update meeting, the following conversation took place:

Riya: My team was able to meet the target in mere three days.

Zoya: Three days? Did you hear that? You can very well understand what quality of work would be done by the team.

In an attempt to outshine colleagues in front of others, people start ambushing. Ambushers listen very attentively to trick the speaker by putting words into their mouths to demonstrate their superiority. Ambushers listen with the objective of gathering details with which the speaker can be targeted. They always look for opportunities to ensnare the speaker in their own words with an aim to prove the speaker wrong.

How Can Active Listening Help You Crack Interviews

You are ready with the best clothing and the most updated resume, but wait! Are you prepared for active listening? Active listening is the key ingredient in determining your success at the interview. Listening actively will keep you focused and make you the most preferred candidate. Generally, before an interview, you toil day and night preparing answers to potential questions. You focus on knowing and remembering the right answers. You deal with the 'what' and 'how', so to speak. In the process, you overlook the most important aspect of active listening.

Active listening is vital to success in an interview. When you actively listen to the question, you tend to understand the underlying meaning and read between the lines. Interviewers are trying to see where you fit in their organization, and by listening, you actually give an impression of your leadership skills and team spirit. Very often, you are able to manage your impression effectively when you listen and comprehend what is said as well as what is not said. In fact, active listening proves instrumental in facilitating your ability to ask the right questions and seek clarifications from the interviewer, if needed.

When you listen actively, you are able to not only give the correct responses but also manage your impression before the interviewers, who are expecting you to be a good communicator. And we have already discussed that 'an effective listener is an impressive communicator.' Active listening combined with the sensible use of non-verbal communication and preparedness pave the way to success in interviews.

In a Nutshell: The Ten Commandments

1. **Follow the 70:30 formula.** Make it a point that no matter how long you are with someone, you will spend 70 percent of the total time listening and 30 percent speaking. Listening is a gift, so gift some of your time to the speaker. You will be remembered for a long time! Moreover, you gain

information, ideas, perspectives, and relationships by listening.

2. **Don't be hyper-receptive;** it will cause information overload. Focus on the idea or theme and ignore minor details and mundane words. Make productive use of selective listening.

3. **Listen with your eyes, too.** Along with what is being said, concentrate on how it is being said. Watch closely the non-verbal behaviour of the speaker to know their emotional intent and feelings. Read between the lines and listen to what is not said as well.

4. **Practice FOLER.** Face the person you are listening to, adopt an open posture, lean slightly, maintain eye contact, and relax.

5. **Detach.** Detach thoughts and ideas from the speaker. Don't let the speaker's traits and aura influence you. Give more importance to what and how something is said rather than who said it.

6. **Do away with filters.** You will be able to communicate with objectivity only when you are able to listen without biases and prejudices. Keep your assumptions, beliefs, and perceptions away while listening.

7. **Remain calm.** Sentiments and emotions often colour the perception and meaning of what is said. They lead to flaming, which leads you to behave under the influence of your emotions and makes you too excited or too angry while listening. Be

in control of your nerves by remaining calm; it facilitates effective listening.

8. **Engage with the speaker.** This helps you listen effectively. Ask questions, clarify doubts, and paraphrase so that you keep yourself away from the non-listening behaviours.

9. **Keep the bigger picture in mind.** Refrain from interrupting the speaker and demonstrate empathy by remaining detached from the speaker's emotional outbursts. The speaker may not feel elated after speaking to you, but he or she should not feel offended either.

10. **Take notes.** Notes can be taken mentally or on paper. During meetings and discussions, use paper; in every other situation, take mental notes while listening.

3

You Are Always Communicating

Nonverbal communication is an elaborate secret code that is written nowhere, known by none, and understood by all.

—Edward Sapir

You have recently joined an organization. Today is the first meeting you are attending. A colleague enters the room after you. He walks sloppily, is dressed clumsily, and moves rubbing past you to a seat. A thought flashes through your mind: 'How careless and ill-mannered!'

Then the CEO walks into the meeting room. He is wearing a branded shirt and trouser, an expensive watch, carrying the latest cell phone, and adorning a costly fragrance. The way he carries himself is worth noticing. You are awestruck. A thought flashes through your mind: 'What a class!'

The thoughts that flashed through your mind are the first impressions that you formed of your colleague and your boss. You did not form the first impression deliberately; it is involuntary by nature and just gets formed. So you see, first impressions are outcomes of largely non-verbal communication. We are told that we don't get a second chance to make a first impression. It is true because, unfortunately, people judge us and form opinions about us based on their first impressions, which is wrong; nonetheless, it happens.

Before we delve into the topic, let me caution you about two things related to non-verbal communication. First, remember that non-verbal communication is very culture-sensitive. What is fine in one culture may be offensive in another, and vice versa. Second, keep in mind that non-verbal communication is a combination of several aspects. Please do not form an opinion about anyone based on one aspect of non-verbal communication.

'Verbal' comes from 'words', so non-verbal is the absence of words, both written and spoken. The 'what' is to be said through words, but the 'how' accounts for the non-verbal, which includes your body language, voice modulation, eye contact, dressing style, behaviour, and what not.

Why Non-Verbal Communication?

Steve Jobs was endowed with indisputable charm, and his appeal was largely because of his eye contact. In a board meeting or while launching a product, the way he looked at people won half the game for him. We all still remember that when he introduced the first iPhone, he ruled the stage with his presence. His walk on the stage and his regal pace added to his excellent eye contact and won the audience. Jobs knew the importance of non-verbal communication and used it to his benefit during his stay on earth.

Combined with words, non-verbal communication makes your message stronger and clearer. You can use it to stress out, support, and cheer up your communication with others. When you communicate, you want others to understand what you intended when you communicated. That's where non-verbal communication plays a crucial role.

Reiteration

Non-verbal communication facilitates reiteration. When you are happy and your body shows it, then people around you feel the vibrations. If your body language is otherwise, then your presence won't motivate anyone.

Paradox

Non-verbal communication is paradoxical as well. It may be contrary to the words used. Suppose you ask someone how they are, and the response is that they are good, but you see tension in their face.

Replacement

There are times when verbal communication can be completely done away with. Silence speaks more than words. Traffic signals, buzzers, and bells signify well-known things that we all comprehend.

Supplementary

Non-verbal communication supplements words. When you are angry, your body language also indicates your anger. Your facial expressions, gestures, and body movements complement your emotion.

Emphasizing

Non-verbal communication facilitates emphasis while interacting. In fact, it carries more power than words alone. When you show a person the direction to a place, you also point your finger towards it, which emphasizes your suggestion.

Similarly, when you are happy for someone, you express your appreciation with words and applaud by clapping your hands.

Mastering Non-Verbal Communication

Kinesics

Kinesics, also known as body language, includes messages through your facial expressions, body movements, including head, torso, and leg movements; gestures; and posture.

Facial Expressions

Facial expressions have the potential to demonstrate every human emotion: happiness, anger, sadness, contempt, surprise, fear, etc. Emotions are inbuilt in the human system, so facial expressions are involuntary. Your body is an asset you have, so ensure you use body language to create a positive impact. Be genuine in whatever you communicate through words, and you will observe that the facial expressions fall into place automatically. Listen attentively, and your facial expressions will complement that: your eyebrows will be slightly raised to show your interest, you will face the speaker to show you are listening, and your nods will indicate you are following what is being shared. In short, if you are happy, you can't fake sadness. The spark in your eyes will say it all.

Gestures

Get involved in what you are saying through words, and spontaneous gestures will follow to emphasize the idea or emotion. Using gestures stresses your point. However, be careful not to over-gesture since that may be distracting. Be composed and do not let your emotions rule you, or else it will result in energetic gestures, which are again distracting. Avoid gestures such as pointing fingers, rubbing hands, and folded arms.

I usually follow this: Be involved in what you communicate! Own your communication, and effective body language flows easily!

Posture

The way you stand and sit says a lot about your confidence and poise. Stand up with shoulders straight and chin level (neither up nor bent) with feet apart (ideally, six inches). Walk at a balanced pace, neither rushing nor sluggarding. Sit with feet on the floor and visible arms and hands, either on the arms of the chair or on your lap. You would definitely not want to give the impression of low energy or a lack of confidence.

I usually follow this: Walk and sit with your head held high and your chin up to the level of the ground! Anything else is unfavourable!

Paralinguistics

Paralinguistics, also known as paralanguage, includes messages through your voice modulation, volume and pitch variation, speaking speed, proper word stress, pauses, and non-fluencies.

Voice Modulation

You are attending a seminar where two speakers are sharing their views. One of them starts and ends in a similar tone, and at the time he spoke, you and others in the audience either dozed off or kept looking at the watch for his talk to conclude. This is a familiar incident, isn't it? Then comes the next speaker, whose voice is full of energy and whose every word you feel is spoken to you personally. You are able to remember most of the things shared by the speaker, and when the talk concludes, you have lost count of time. You realize you have been mesmerized. That is what voice modulation—the rising and falling tone—can do to an interaction or a talk. When you are in control of the rising and falling tone of your voice, you are able to catch your listener's attention with a minor dramatic effect while speaking. How can you modulate your voice? Simple. Believe in what you are saying. Voice modulation also helps your listeners pay attention to what you are saying. Suppose you are in a meeting and there is a heated debate over something, and your opinion is solicited. When you start opining, begin with a rising tone to take charge of the situation, then use the falling tone to add effect, and use the right combination of the rising and falling tone according to the topic at hand.

Volume and Pitch Variation

The loudness with which you speak affects your communication. Learn to adjust the volume of your voice according to the size of the audience. Volume variation is also important during telephonic conversations. Pitch variation refers to the frequency of sound while speaking. Ensure there is no shrillness in your voice. Conflicts and quarrels are generally outcomes of shrillness in the voice, which makes you appear to be screaming. So mind the variations in volume and pitch.

Speaking Speed

How often have you come across someone who said something and you realized you did not understand a word? And how often have you heard someone start speaking, and you waited for it to get over? That's precisely what happens when the speaking speed is either too fast or too slow. Speak at a normal speed, taking the necessary pauses in between to give your listener/audience time to absorb and reflect upon what you said. Take non-verbal cues from them and adjust your speaking speed.

Proper Word Stress

Stress on different words of the same sentence can change its meaning. Let's take this example: We are working this Saturday.

When the first word 'we' is stressed, the underlying message is that only your team is working this Saturday. The stress on 'are' indicates that there is no way to escape from working this Saturday. The stress on 'working' shows that your team is working and not doing anything else this Saturday. The stress on 'this' signifies that your team is working just this Saturday. The stress on Saturday demonstrates surprise, shock, sadness, happiness, etc., based on the facial expressions used along with the word stress.

Basically, the stress you apply to words or sentences shows how much emphasis you are placing on the word or sentence.

Improper stress has the potential to distort the meaning of the sentence and cause confusion and misunderstanding.

Pauses

Pauses refer to a momentary stop while communicating. These are either silent or filled with words or sounds. These are of different lengths. These may be voluntary or involuntary. Voluntary pauses are effective and boost the delivery of the message, while involuntary pauses may confuse and amuse the receivers.

Pause, when used properly, allows you to draw together your thoughts and ideas and deliver them with rejuvenation. A purposeful pause after sharing a thought equips your listener to grasp the message. It can also develop excitement, leading to interest. A brief pause just before concluding what you are saying is an effective way of ensuring active listening. Pause after each thought and before beginning something new, just like you use commas and full stops in writing.

As stated above, some pauses are filled with words or sounds. These fillers include 'um', 'err', 'argh', 'grunts', 'well', 'you know', 'I mean', the repetition of the last word at the beginning of a new sentence, etc. Some sounds, such as 'um' and 'err', come naturally while you are trying to recall an incident; however, some sounds and words result from our habits and lack of vocabulary.

Non-fluencies

Involuntary use of sounds and words comes naturally in some circumstances, which is understood by the receiver. However, when the receiver starts counting the words you are using while pausing, the essence of your message is lost. These days, you will find yourself and people around you using the following fillers frequently while talking:

- You know
- Basically
- Actually
- So
- OK
- Right
- I mean

You must be wondering that these are words; why have we included them in non-verbal communication? The answer is because they are not used to represent their literal meaning when used as a filler word. For example:

Your colleague meets you after a week's leave and initiates a discussion with you, saying, 'You know what happened when I went to Goa last Friday . . .'

How are you expected to know what happened when she went to Goa last Friday unless she shares it with you?

I usually follow this: Rather than a discourse, speak in a conversational mode; paralanguage will be taken care of without much effort!

Oculesics

This includes messages through your eye contact. Direct eye contact, indirect eye contact, and duration of eye contact constitute oculesics. The signals we give through the way we maintain eye contact say tons about our credibility and behaviour. Some other forms of eye contact include staring (gazing), withdrawing eye contact, and having too little eye contact.

Eye contact is an indicator of active listening, interest, and availability while communicating. The acceptance of direct and indirect eye contact differs from culture to culture. While some cultures (e.g., Western) may interpret direct eye contact (looking into the eyes) as honesty, others (e.g., African) may associate lowering of the eyes while communicating with humility, while still others (e.g., Middle Eastern) may perceive it as showing interest.

Having said this, you should remember that your ideal eye contact may come to your rescue in most cultures. The duration of ideal eye contact is around three seconds. Ensure you don't look behind the ears of the speaker, at the nose of the speaker, or fix your gaze into the eyes of the speaker. The zone should be between the tips of the eyebrows on either side, the centre of the forehead, and the eyes of the speaker. Remember, eye contact for more than three seconds is enough to daunt or overwhelm the speaker, affecting the speaker's confidence.

I usually follow this: Look at people the way you are comfortable with people looking at you!

Proxemics

This includes messages sent through the use of space or distance while communicating. The message you give through the space you use and the distance you maintain while interacting depends a lot on which culture you belong to and whom you are interacting with. Edward Hall introduced the concept of proxemics, along with its four types, way back in the 1960s in his book *The Silent Language*. He identified four zones when it comes to proxemics: intimate, personal, social, and public.

1. Intimate zone comprises space from body touch (e.g., hug) to the distance you require to whisper (0–18 inches). Although there is touch in a handshake, the zone is not intimate since you maintain distance.

2. Personal zones range from 18 inches to 4 feet. This is the space you are most of the time in while communicating with family and friends, in a cafeteria, sometimes while signing documents, etc. This personal zone sometimes gets encroached upon in elevators, crowds, trains, buses, queues, escalators, etc. As long as this encroachment is natural and unintentional, one is fine with it. The moment one realizes it is intentional, one becomes uncomfortable. Many deals are unable to get through because wrong opinions are formed based on the encroachment of the personal zone.

3. The social zone ranges from 4–10 feet. This is the space you are most of the time in while

communicating with colleagues at work, in a meeting, etc. If colleagues encroach into each other's personal zone, they give the wrong signal to people around them even before they realize it. So be careful!

4. The public zone is above 10 feet. This is the space used in public speaking. Ensure you adjust your volume and body language while communicating in a public zone.

Culture and personal attributes play an important role in proxemics. Sometimes, one may encroach on your personal zone because of the culture one comes from, where encroaching on the personal zone is considered being close and trustworthy (e.g., the Middle East). On the other hand, you may be perceived as being pushy if you enter personal space (e.g., the USA).

You must be wondering why you cannot carry a measuring tape while dealing with people. Yes, you cannot; however, a mental measurement of distance makes things easier. In case you find someone behaving contrary to how the distances should be followed, try to understand why the person is behaving in that manner. Don't judge.

I usually follow this: While determining what distance you should maintain while communicating, the formula is simple: don't intimidate the receiver!

Haptics

Haptics is what you communicate through the way you touch. Touch effectively communicates feelings and sends out the signal of trust if done and perceived in the right spirit. However, in the absence of the right spirit, the same touch can cause a breach of trust. Haptics comprises pats, hugs, handshakes, kisses, slaps, etc. Every form of touch has a meaning, like love, intimacy, friendship, motivation, violence, and gratitude, among others. Touch and its interpretations vary from person to person and are based on situations such as the workplace, personal, professional, friendship, and greeting, to name a few. Haptics is the most effective way of communicating because touch strengthens bonds and develops rapport. Nonetheless, you need to be cautious while using haptics and listen to your instinct before touching.

Your colleague has done an excellent job on the report she has prepared, and as the team leader, you genuinely want to give her a pat on the shoulder and congratulate her. On another occasion, a colleague comes and informs you that you bagged the big deal that you were waiting for, and you get so overwhelmed that you just want to give him a hug. Hold on. Motivating a team member with a pat on the shoulder and sharing moments of success with a colleague are fine as long as they are perceived the way you intend.

I usually follow this: 'Whenever in doubt, don't touch!'

Handshake

We live in a competitive world, and the first impression is what makes you unique. This begins with a handshake. I will walk you through some types of handshakes and share how you might deal with them. At times, handshakes result from one's prejudice, ego, position, inferiority complex, and other psychological reasons.

While shaking hands, don't discriminate based on gender or other factors while initiating a handshake. Any gender may initiate a handshake with any gender. Let the person in the most senior position initiate the handshake, no matter how modern and open your workplace is. Why? It is quite embarrassing if your handshake is not reciprocated. Avoid shaking hands with wet palms. Use one hand to hold your drink to keep the other free for a handshake. Try to use an ideal handshake to avoid misperceptions about your behaviour.

There are many types of 'shakes' that you can't drink!

Ideal

This is the one you should use with everyone you plan to shake hands with. Here, the palms of both persons are parallel to each other, fingers are clasped nicely, thumbs are in perfect grip, maintaining a smile and warmth on the face, you give two-three pumps before withdrawing your hand. This type of handshake is successful and does not leave any room for misunderstanding.

Glove (Politician)

It is generally used by politicians or someone patronizing you. After holding your hand to shake, the person covers your hand with the other hand.

Royal

In this type of handshake, a person just touches your fingers and makes you feel royal. The message intended here is that you are gentle, so touched in this manner. This is outdated, although those in health profession do use it for hygienic purposes. In all other cases, it should be avoided.

Bone Crusher/Knuckle Cruncher

Persons using this handshake often seek pleasure in displaying their strength. In the process, they hold your hand with such force that you might feel your bones crushing or your knuckles crunching with the power.

Dominating

In this handshake, after initiating the handshake, the person puts your hand down. This handshake is, generally, the result of position or the power one enjoys. This is a symbol of dominance.

Submissive

In this handshake, after initiating the handshake, the person puts your hand up. This handshake is, generally, the result of inferiority complex. This is a symbol of submission.

Dead Fish (Limp)

This handshake feels like you are holding a dead fish and comes from those who are uninterested, unexcited or afraid while greeting you.

Lingering

It is when a person shakes your hand and doesn't let go. It is lingering, goes on and on and you find yourselves helpless in most cases because abruptly pulling away your hand looks rude to you.

High Five and Fist Bump

These are used to show camaraderie or acknowledge in semiformal and informal situations.

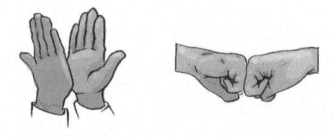

I usually follow this: Ideal handshake is not open to people's perceptions! Follow it!

Chronemics

Chronemics deals with what messages you deliver by how you follow time. You can use time to communicate how punctual you are about response times, your willingness to wait, and time management as a whole. It was Edward Hall who indicated that there are two basic segments that cultures may be divided into—monochronic and polychronic.

The following table discusses the differences succinctly.

Monochronic	Polychronic
Follow time as a linear concept	Follow time as a spiral concept
One task at a time	Many things together
Job/work focused	Easily distracted
Dislike borrowing or lending things	Borrow and lend very often
Timelines are sacrosanct	Timelines are easy and flexible
Dedicated and loyal to work	Dedicated and loyal to people
Stick to plans made	Change plans easily and frequently
Written word of more value	Word of mouth is enough
Concentrate more on verbal communication	Concentrate more on nonverbal communication
Negotiations quick and based on facts	Negotiations take long time and are based on relationships
Timeliness and punctuality of utmost importance, always	Timeliness and punctuality least important and vary
Germany, UK, Turkey, Japan, Switzerland, Canada	Africa, South Asia, the Arab region

I usually follow this: Get sensitized to a foreign culture while on an overseas work or leisure trip!

Chromatics

Chromatics involves your messages through the way you use colour. Colours speak for themselves. For example, black indicates mourning; white is a symbol of purity and peace and is used in some weddings, while it is used in some cultures as a symbol of sadness and death; purple indicates royalty; red stands for stop or danger; yellow is a sign of getting ready; green signifies go or environment. The use of colours varies across cultures. Organizations express their organizational culture through different colours. In fact, office space in different colours demonstrates joy at work.

You give signals to people by the colour of the clothes you wear during meetings, social gatherings, and other occasions. Your choice of colour displays your sensitivity to the people and cultures you interact with.

I usually follow this: Understand the culture if it is different from yours while choosing colours!

Olfactics

Olfactics includes the messages you give through your sense of smell. Every person has two smells to handle: natural body odour and breath. Natural body odour should be preferably concealed with a suitable smell or fragrance. Generally, you use perfumes and deodorants to hide body odour. No matter what you use, ensure the fragrance covers your body odour without disturbing the noses of people around you. Perfumes and deodorants both do the same thing, but with the difference that perfumes, even the mildest, may reach others' noses while deodorants, even the strongest, stay on you.

I usually follow this: Use your perfumes at get-togethers, parties or networking events. However, make sure you use the strongest deodorant while at work. With regard to foul breath, maintain oral hygiene. If the problem persists, use a mouth freshener. Do not keep chewing gum at all times!

Silence

As the name indicates, silence is what you say when you don't speak. You can give several non-verbal messages through silence with the right combination of various facial expressions and body movements to express anger, disagreement, agreement, contempt, frustration, overwhelming emotion, fear, etc.

Silence will make you more effective in the following situations:

While negotiating: It is advisable to use silence while negotiating. It motivates the other person to express more than they intended, leading you to refrain from reacting. Listening silently gives you the power position, indicating that the other person needs the transaction more than you do. Of course, your facial expressions, eye contact and posture should complement your silence.

While presenting: When you find speaking before a large audience unnerving, resort to the meaningful use of silence to gain control over your anxiety and the audience. Combine slowing your speaking speed with pauses and silence to make your presentation effective. Silent pauses before or after critical statements while presenting add value to what you are saying and also enhance your executive presence. Use silence to gather your thoughts logically before responding to questions after the presentation. When used at the right spots, silence while presenting has a positive impact on your credibility.

While attending meetings: Everyone is in talk mode during meetings and, in that mode, misses out on listening to other people's concerns and suggestions. Choose to be silent and see the magic! You will find the quiet members of your team speaking, and your team will become more thoughtful and creative.

While working across cultures: While working across cultures, remember that they might not be well versed in English and may take longer to understand and reply. Remain silent, thereby allowing them space to interpret your messages and frame their responses.

I usually follow this: Silence may be easily misunderstood if accompanied with incorrect body language. So use it wisely!

How Non-Verbal Communication Can Go Wrong

Remember, non-verbal communication is subconscious. It may deliver confusing signals if not used consciously. Improper non-verbal communication may lead to a loss of trust and credibility.

Let's explore Shanaya, your team leader. Shanaya shares a very friendly relationship with the team members. She believes that her team likes her. However, the team members get uncomfortable the moment Shanaya talks to them. Her gaze, while talking, disturbs the team. They find it piercing and avoid looking at her while she is talking. Shanaya is a good leader but not liked by her team. Her gaze forces people to keep their distance from her.

Then there is a colleague of yours, Roy, who crunches palm bones and crushes others' fingers while shaking hands. He speaks loudly in a high pitch. His routine verbal exchange appears like a quarrel to the others. When Roy shakes hands the way he does, he feels he is displaying warmth. When he is speaking loudly and in a high pitch, he feels he is being enthusiastic. Unfortunately, people are not taking the message he intends to give.

To avoid the aforesaid goof-ups, stay away from misunderstandings, and advance professionally and socially, it is important to polish your non-verbal communication skills as much as your verbal communication. In fact, you should control your non-verbal messages, and they will help you give the right message, positive or negative.

Non-Verbal Communication at an Interview

Preparing for an Interview

Usually, you want to prepare for the interview so that you can give the best answers possible to the questions they ask. Your focus is largely on the 'what', but remember that without the 'how' the 'what' may not create an impact. Your best verbal response is the 'cake,' and your best non-verbal communication is the 'icing on the cake'. You want them both perfect, don't you?

Prepare how you will say the answers with the right body language and paralanguage as you work on the answers. While preparing, focus on your facial expressions, gestures, speaking speed, and voice modulation. Your posture while sitting in a chair makes a big difference. Prepare in front of the mirror or video record your mock interview with the help of a friend and improve your non-verbal communication after reviewing the recording and seeking feedback from the friend.

Non-verbal communication is important right from the moment you step into the interview room. The way you enter the room, hesitatingly or confidently, has started creating your first impression in the interviewers' minds. Ensure you are dressed decently. You do not need to buy expensive, branded clothes every time you appear for an interview. Your hygiene, accompanied by clean and ironed clothes and proper footwear, is enough evidence of your credibility. Avoid smoking, chewing gum, and using strong perfumes—they might very well spoil your chances even before the interview.

During the Interview

- Sit in a composed posture, maintaining frequent eye contact with the interviewer.
- Have warmth on your face.
- Politeness is required, but don't overdo it.
- Be confident and let your body show it. Keep your posture open. Sit with a slight lean forward to appear interested.
- Avoid fidgeting with a pen or folder, your palm, or your fingers.
- Listen without interrupting.

- Read the non-verbal communication of the interviewer.

- Maintain your cool. Stress interviews are meant to stress you. Relax. Control your emotions and respond calmly to the nastiest questions asked.

- Your facial expressions and gestures should complement your words. Don't over-gesture and keep away from energy gestures.

- Nod when needed.

- Even when responding to the question asked by one interviewer, maintain eye contact with all of them, with more focus on the interviewer who asked the question without ignoring the rest.

- Use voice modulation when required and stress key words and points.

- Sit with your arms on the chair or on your lap.

- Avoid touching your face and doing your hair during the interview.

- Thank the interviewers with a smile on your face after the interview.

Non-Verbal Communication When Hiring

Many a time, it has happened that you have differentiated between two candidates with equal expertise and experience based on the attitude and approach one of them demonstrated even without speaking. While wearing the interviewer's hat, ensure you evaluate a candidate based on a combination of verbal and non-verbal communication. Evaluating a candidate's non-verbal communication will assist you in finding the right fit for your organization's culture and setting.

Initial Glance

Does the candidate appear confident in the way she walks into the interview venue and in the manner in which she pulls the chair to occupy it? Are the facial muscles relaxed? These are important hints for you to gauge the candidate's composure at this juncture.

How does the candidate appear the moment she or he enters the interview room? Does the walk demonstrate confidence, or is there a lack of confidence? The smile on the candidate's face exhibits energy and zeal for the position applied for. As an interviewer, don't be quick to judge. Just because the candidate is not wearing a watch, it does not mean the person is not brilliant. While deciding on the appropriateness of the candidate, evaluate the non-verbal aspects as a whole and not in isolation.

Body Language

Does the candidate sit with shoulders drooping? Or is the candidate relaxed? What are the facial expressions and gestures while responding to the questions? Are the head nods, facial expressions, and gestures just right, or are they overdone or absent? Keep a close watch on the energy level. Does the candidate display confidence in shaking hands?

Appearance

Assess the candidate's choice of professional appearance, right from the way the hair is done to the suitable attire to the footwear to the perfume to the accessories one is carrying, which include the folder and pen, among others.

Eye Contact

Observe the candidate's eye contact with you and others in the interview panel. Is it a gaze or withdrawal of eyes—frequent, very less frequent, missing completely, or just as needed? Does the candidate appear interested during the interview? Or searches the room with eyes? Or simply looks behind your ears or shoulders? Or looks at your nose? Certainly, these behaviours are uncalled for and make it easy for you to decide. After all, you are bringing another colleague on board.

In a Nutshell

After this journey of understanding non-verbal communication, you might have very well realized its importance. You say a lot without saying it, and so does your audience. Not only is it significant to mind your non-verbal communication, but it is also crucial for you to understand the non-verbal communication of your audience.

4

Wielding the Pen

Writing is easy. All you have to do is to cross out the wrong words.

— **Mark Twain**

Seven Canons of Eloquent Writing

In today's world, where communication has become the key word, we always express ourselves through writing in addition to speaking. Our writing in our professional space is either as texts or emails or reports or business marketing proposals, and so on. Hence, it becomes imperative on our part to wield the pen with power. This power comes from the ammunition of canons, which serve to strengthen our writing. Let's get empowered with these canons of eloquent writing.

Canon 1: Use Correct and Simple Words

Words have denotative and connotative meanings. While denotative meaning is literal with different shades and explicit in nature, connotative meaning is subjective, contextual, and implicit in nature. Not every connotation is only positive or negative; it may be neutral based on how it is used. Use connotations to set the right tone and explain your intent; however, remember that the choice of the wrong connotation may actually develop an unsought reaction and lead to misinterpreted intent. Even with denotative meanings, there might be confusion regarding similar-sounding words such as appraise and apprise, and compliment and complement. On the other hand, the connotative meaning of slim may vary based on the past experiences of the sender and receiver. Hence, try to use as few words as possible with a single meaning.

Let's look at the following examples of connotation.

Positive	Neutral	Negative
Employ	Use	Exploit
Thrifty	Saving	Miserly
Unique	Different	Peculiar
Elated	Happy	Frenzied
Vintage	Old	Dilapidated

Canon 2: Use Short Words and Phrases

In the busy environment in which most of us work, it is very important to use short words and phrases so as not to sound like we are beating around the bush. Such words are not only succinct in nature but also indicate your clarity of thought.

In Place of	Use
At the present time	Now
Owing to the fact that	Because
By means of	By
In the vicinity	Near
With regard to	Regarding
Terminate	End
Usage	Use
Modification	Change
Rendezvous	Meeting

Wordy: We received your inquiry that you wrote about badminton rackets yesterday.

Concise: We received your inquiry about badminton rackets yesterday.

Wordy: After booking a ticket to New York from a travel agent, she packed her luggage and hired a taxi to the airport. Once there, she checked in, went through security, and was ready to board. But due to issues that were not foreseen, there was a five-hour delay before takeoff.

Concise: Her flight to New York was delayed for five hours.

Canon 3: Use Specific Words

Your goal when writing should never be to confuse the reader with words that aren't clear. Conversely, it should be to use specific words indicating concrete meanings.

In Place of	Use
In the near future	By Thursday, 27 December
A significant margin	A 15% margin
I enjoyed the class.	I enjoyed the first class in the morning by Kim.
He is an intelligent student.	He earned the highest marks in term I in a class of 70 students.
Substantial increase in prices	10% increase in prices

Canon 4: Avoid Redundant Words

Redundancy proves futile in every business transaction, including written communication. To avoid redundancy, try to understand words before using them.

In Place of	Use
Revert back	Revert
True facts	Facts
In order to	To
Close proximity	Proximity
Major breakthrough	Breakthrough

In Place of	Use
Sum total	Sum/total
Consensus of opinion	Consensus
At a later time	Later
Within a period of one year	Within one year
Basic principles	Principles

Canon 5: Say No to Clichés and Jargon

Refrain from clichés and jargon to make understanding easier for your receiver.

In Place of	Use
Busy as a bee	Busy
Rock of Gibraltar	Reliable
Down to earth	Realistic/practical
Smart as a whip	Intelligent
White as snow	Clean/pure/white

Jargon	Layperson's Meaning
Assessed valuation	Value of the property for tax purposes
The helicopter view	Overall sketch
Brick and mortar	Physical location
Burn the compact disc (CD)	Make a copy on CD
Hammer it out	To type something up
Drill down	Analyse
Pull the trigger	Initiate

Canon 6: Use Positive and Non-Discriminatory Words

Whether you are talking to a senior or a junior, an internal or an external stakeholder, positive words lead to positive results.

Negative: I cannot complete the project report by tomorrow morning.

Positive: I can complete the project report only by 2.30 p.m. tomorrow.

Negative: You should not use Form 22 to file the monthly target achieved report.

Positive: Form 20 is the monthly target achieved report.

Discriminatory	Non-discriminatory
Man hours	Work hours
Salesman	Salesperson
Chairman	Chairperson/Chair
Mrs or Miss	Ms
Authoress	Author
A Chinese teacher	A teacher
Mankind	Humankind

Canon 7: Use Active Voice

Use the active voice to deliver a message effectively. Active voice strengthens the sentence and emphasizes the doer of the action, while passive voice weakens the sentence because it emphasizes the action and not the doer.

Active: Rocky led the meeting.

Passive: The meeting was led by Rocky.

Active: Rhea won the 'best employee' award.

Passive: The best employee award was won by Rhea.

Active: The new author reorganized the manuscript.

Passive: A reorganization of the manuscript was done by the new author.

Although you should prefer active voice most of the time, passive voice without the definite article 'by' may be used occasionally for diplomatic and sensitive purposes where the doer of the action is better removed.

Active: The purchase director sought bids from local vendors.

Passive: Bids from local vendors were sought.

Lastly, Don't Forget the 'First-You' Attitude

All forms of writing give the desired outcome when they are filled with attitude. Your attitude in writing means to be reader-focused. It is vital to keep in mind that a number of readers have an objective of 'How do I benefit?' tangibly or intangibly, or 'How does it reduce my problem?' In short, 'What's in it for me?' Catering to this objective yields desirable results. Therefore, while communicating in positive circumstances, try to expand the positive effect of the news. In negative circumstances, try to decrease the negative effect while emphasizing the reader's benefits. For instance, if the credit manager of a business writes to collect the due payments from the customer, it is an absence of attitude. However, if the credit manager stresses the point that payment of dues will ensure the customer preserves all benefits from the store along with a good credit rating, this will have a far better effect than the previous one with a no-you attitude.

Error-free and simple messages cater to the needs of your attitude. Avoid sentences that begin with 'I', 'me' or 'mine', as well as 'we', 'us' and 'our/ours'. It is advisable to focus on 'you' and 'yours'. Instead of saying, 'We are sending the samples of our new cosmetic products,' choose to write, 'You will receive the samples of our new cosmetic products.'

Forms of Written Organizational Communication

Business letters, emails, reports, proposals, memos, etc., constitute written organizational communication. In addition to the seven Cs of communication and the seven canons of eloquent writing, there are certain major aspects that should be considered while writing for the desired outcome.

Emails and memos are brief forms of communication, because of which we often ignore writing them with diligence. We feel these are just for sharing information, so we do not need to waste our time thinking about how to write them. Conversely, these are the most sensitive in carrying the messages and should be handled with delicacy.

Proper Panning Leads to Effective Messages

Who (receiver): Be clear about whom you are writing to. Write it as you would like to read it.

What (subject): Be specific about the subject matter you want to deal with in the piece of writing. It includes the subject line as well as the body of the message, divided into paragraphs.

How (delivery): Be formal and professional in the way you write. In other words, adjust the tone of your message to the subject you are writing on.

Memo

A memorandum, which is called a memo, is a form of internal organizational communication sent for routine matters by someone who the receiver is acquainted with. For this reason, it does not follow formalities such as a salutation or a complimentary close. Memos are written to give or ask information, share a new policy, provide an update on transfers and other internal matters, advocate an action to solve a problem, persuade and share suggestions with senior officials. Memos are generally written in two to three brief paragraphs.

Elements of an Effective Memo

An effective memo catches the eye of the receiver, gives complete information, calls for action, recommends, discusses advantages to the reader, and directs the course of action and timelines.

Like every other form of writing, compose the memo following the given steps:

1. **Plan:** Have a clear idea of the purpose of writing the memo.
2. **Draft:** Create a draft of your memo.
3. **Revise:** Revise for clarity, better understanding, and tone.
4. **Edit:** Edit wherever required.

Major Parts: Heading and Body

Heading:
To: Receiver/s of the memo
From: Sender of the memo
Date: On which the memo is sent
Subject: Crisp and concise subject line

Body:
Introduction
Facts
Relevance of facts
Conclusion (including call for action)

After the following elements, it comes straight to the point:

From _____　　　Subject _____
To _____　　　　Date _____

Another way of putting this could be:

To: _____　　　　Date: _____
From: _____
Subject: _____

Following are the examples of memos used in business.

Memo 1

ABG Corporation
Internal Memorandum

To: All employees
From: Amrita Tiwari, Transport In-Charge
Date: 14 June 2021

Subject: Misuse of office shuttle-bus service

In view of the rising fuel costs, we have revised our policy on the use of the office shuttlebus service. Our policy, at present, does not allow the use of the office shuttle-bus service for personal use due to the soaring costs of fuel. We understand that this may not be a suitable resolution, so employees can now use the office shuttle-bus service by paying for each trip.

The cost of using the service has been posted on notice boards.

Memo 2

To: All supervisors
From: Ronny Fernandes, Vice-President, Marketing
Date: 28 June 2021
Subject: Update on marketing strategy for Parley-T

As informed in April, we received a one-year contract from Parley-T to develop a new marketing strategy for their product for the rural areas.

Our team has since then made every effort to get the best of strategies to stand true to the customer's expectations. The strategy will be presented in our company auditorium to all our employees before delivering it to the customer on 1 July 2021, 4 p.m. Attendance is compulsory.

An evaluation sheet will be circulated after the presentation for your inputs on the strategy presented. I will revert in a week's time after collating the inputs with the revised strategy incorporating those.

Both the sample memos are:

- Crisp and brief
- Simple
- Courteous
- With you-attitude

Email

We all have fallen in love with social networking and prefer it over email as a means of communication. However, email still remains valuable in business. This is largely because exchanging emails is convenient. Moreover, emails are prevalent due to their universal acceptance, their importance in keeping records, and the fact that they can be used as evidence in a court of law. Emails also have the feature of allowing you to engage with your receiver on a personal level while maintaining professionalism.

Format for Emails

1. Subject line
2. Salutation
3. The message
4. Complimentary close (optional)
5. Name of the sender
6. Contact information

Subject Lines

Have you ever received an email with such a predictable subject line that you did not open it? Do you promptly open the emails that have neutral subject lines? In fact, the very subject line douses or ignites your excitement. See what a major role the subject line has in an email! It has the capacity to make or break a deal or relationship. Your subject line should be crisp, to the point, and not more than eight words. Use only universally accepted abbreviations and acronyms in the subject line. Wherever necessary, use EOM (end of message) in the subject line.

Let's see an example here.

You sent the following email to your team on 10 December 2020.

> Subject line: Sales team meeting
> Dear colleagues,
>
> The meeting of the sales team has been convened as per the following details to discuss the three items mentioned in the enclosed agenda.
>
> Date: 20 August 2021
> Time: 10–11 am
> Venue: Board Room 1
> Attendance to the meeting is compulsory.
>
> Regards,
> Deepa

You plan to send a reminder to the sales team a day before the meeting. In that case, simply the subject line with EOM will suffice instead of writing the entire message again.

> Subject: Sales team meeting tomorrow, 10–11 am, Board Room 1 (EOM)

EOM indicates to the receiver that it is just a reminder for the next day's meeting and that there is nothing embedded in the message box of the email.

Similarly, one can use the word 'long' in parentheses in the subject line whenever it is a long email, for which the receiver will need time to read. For example, see the following:

> Subject: New HR policy enclosed (long)

If the same subject line endures for a series of exchange, either change the subject line or start a new thread.

For example, Re: Re: Re: Re: Fwd: Re: Fwd: Fwd: Fwd.

Avoid all caps in the subject line as well as the body of the email. It is virtual shouting and amounts to flaming.

Don't use URGENT as the subject line. If it is really that urgent, pick up the phone, write a text message, or send an instant message. In case you have to use it, use it without all caps and sparingly.

For negative messages, use a neutral subject line. If, for example, you are denying a request, don't write 'Denial of request' in the subject line. Use 'regarding your request'. Positive words, on the other hand, may be the subject line of positive messages like 'Congratulations' or 'Best wishes'.

For your peace of mind, do away with the word 'reminder' from your life. Human beings, by nature, love to be reminded, but not with the word reminder.

The word reminder is considered a blow, and softening the blow by adding adjectives like 'gentle', 'friendly' or 'warm' does no good. How many times have you sent emails with a reminder in the subject line and gotten an immediate response? Hardly. Moreover, if the word reminder had really been fruitful, why would you find 'reminder 1, 2, 3, nth'? So the point is that the word 'reminder' does nothing. In fact, you can very well remind people and get things done by reminding them assertively with more powerful but neutral words. For instance, instead of writing a gentle reminder and reiterating the details in the body of the email, you may simply write, Ref: XYZ project report submission timeline tomorrow (EOM).

Salutation

Have you ever wondered how a formal letter would appear without referring to the receiver through a salutation? Emails follow the format of formal letters. The same rule for salutation applies in emails. The right salutation sets the right tone for the email. Most often used salutations include Ma'am or Sir, Dear Ms or Mr XYZ, and Ms or Mr XYZ. Some organizational cultures use 'respected', while bureaucrats still use 'honorable'.

Decide the salutation based on how you are related to the receiver. It is better to be formal than be perceived as having subjectivity when writing salutations. If you are writing an email to someone for the first time, try to find the person's name and title through company websites or professional social networks like LinkedIn. Alternatively, you may scour the website to reach the administrative assistant and call to seek the required details of the person to whom you wish to send the email.

Professional Email Salutation Examples

Use 'dear' if you know the name of the person you are writing to. Use it with the receiver's title. If the title is not known after making all efforts to find it, use Ms. or Mr. followed by the last name. Avoid using titles with the first name. You may use the first name with 'Dear' if you work with the person at a level where you address each other by the first name or if your organizational culture suggests so. Ensure you write out titles like governor, professor, captain, etc. The correct title shows your eye for details and is appreciated. However, the use of an incorrect title may damage your reputation.

Use 'hi' or 'hello' when you are addressing a department or a client or supplier you work closely with and have developed a friendly relationship with. Ensure you begin the name of the recipient with 'hi' or 'hello'. For example, 'Hi Reema' or 'Hello Karan'.

Try to Avoid the Following Salutations

Avoid using 'To whom it may concern.' It is an outdated salutation because, today, the world has come to a click of a button, and not being able to trace the receiver is less likely. Also, it is a very impersonal way of addressing the receiver. If you have no idea about the recipient, use 'hi' or 'hello' or other greetings.

Avoid using 'hey'. It is an informal salutation used in informal emails. This might work among colleagues; however, it seldom works with clients and seniors unless your work culture allows it.

Avoid using 'dear madam' or 'sir' as far as possible. It is outdated and impersonal. Use it as the last option.

Keep away from gendered salutations like 'hey, guys', although it might be a comprehensive phrase with regard to gender.

As a salutation, it isn't suitable. Similar is the case with 'Ladies' and 'Gentlemen'.

No exclamation marks are needed after the salutation. It indicates overwhelming emotions and is far from being professional.

These small considerations go a long way in setting the tone of the email.

Message

Do you appreciate emails with long paragraphs that come to the point after a detailed background and context? Or do you like emails with concise messages? Keep the message short and crisp. Ensure the body of the email comprises not more than three paragraphs: the opening/introduction, main message, and conclusion. If it is going to be longer, enclose a Word or PDF document. Use one email per subject line in order not to cause confusion.

Closing an Email

A salutation is the entrance gate to an email, while its closing is the exit door of the email. Just like the salutation sets the tone of the email, the closing leaves the receiver with a good impression. Your email sign-off (closing and signature) is a very important component of the email. The email's closing is an encouraging feature in how fast your receiver responds, if at all.

Email closure is like ending a conversation. Do you end a conversation by abruptly leaving the place where you were talking to a client, or do you close the conversation politely and leave? Chances of a positive outcome increase with the use of a professional email closing.

Ideal Email Closing/Ending

A closing line:

Include a positive statement in the concluding line that will encourage the receiver to either respond or show that you are awaiting a response.

For example,
I look forward to hearing from you.

Truly,
Ben Jonson

Your Complete Details

Use your full name in your email signature, followed
by your title, designation, organization name, address,
email address, and contact number.

Ned Singh
Marketing Head
ABG Corporation Ltd., New Delhi ned.singh@gmail.
com 111xxx444ccc4
+00-20x-33xxxx66

Complimentary Close

The choice of a complimentary closing depends on
the subject matter in the body of the email. Common
complimentary close words are:

- Thank you
- Thanks and regards
- Sincerely
- Regards

Words like 'warmest regards', 'best wishes' and 'regards' should be used with caution. Configure in your mind if the opposite of that word also makes sense in complimentary close. If the answer is 'no', avoid it. Technically, 'warm regards' and 'best regards' neither make sense nor add to the meaning of regards. Nonetheless, these may be used as rhetoric to add value to what is being said. These words may not denote anything significant, but they surely connote feelings and emotions.

Stay away from complimentary close words like cheers (OK in some cultures only), peace, your buddy, see you, catch you soon, etc.

What Not to Include in the Email Signature

Complimentary close: Remember, this is not a part of your signature. The complimentary close varies according to the body of the message, so it cannot be a part of the email signature.

Quotes: These are not required. The purpose of the email signature is to provide the sender's detailed information, and quotes cannot be a part of it. A quote in the email signature is just out of place.

Preach notes: Refrain from preaching and patronizing. For example, 'Please consider the environment before printing this email.' Come on, everyone is aware of environmental conservation.

Other things to remember while writing emails:

Reply to All: Please don't abuse this feature of the email. Use it only when required and mostly for your information.

CC (carbon copy): Use it with caution and for only those who have some information about what's going on. Don't give a copy to people who are not directly or indirectly connected with the subject. CC does have some political uses where some stakeholders are kept in the loop for certain reasons.

BCC (blind carbon copy): In today's business world, where 'transparency' is the key word, BCC is not in vogue.

Flaming: Keep an arm's length away from flaming. Flaming may include anything from an unfriendly tone and words to abusive language and all caps to offensive language. Maintain email courtesy for a better impact.

Proofread before sending: Once you are done with the first draft, re-read for editing, revising, and proofreading before hitting the send button.

Another important form of written organizational communication is business lettering. Let's take a peek at business letters, which may be typed, printed on the company letterhead, and sent or enclosed with the email as an enclosure (in email language, an attachment). They follow the process discussed in emails.

The major parts include:

1. Sender's address
2. Date
3. Receiver's address
4. Salutation
5. Subject line
6. The message
7. Complimentary close
8. Signature block

Sender's name
Sender's company name
Sender's complete address
Sender's city, state and postal code
Sender's contact number and email address

Date

Receiver's name
Receiver's company name
Receiver's complete address
Receiver's city, state and postal code
Receiver's contact number and email address

Subject

Dear Name,

Introduction—In the first paragraph, you explain the rationale of the letter which includes the reason you are writing it, what is your expected outcome from it and anything else you want to state honestly in the beginning.

Main message—In the middle paragraph, you explain and give more details about the things mentioned in the first paragraph. The main message may have more than one paragraph according to the length of the letter.

Conclusion—In the last paragraph, you recapitulate and conclude all things. Call to action or next steps may be a part of this paragraph.

Sincerely,
Signature
Name of Sender

Business Letter Formats

Block: Block format is the most preferred format for a business letter. In block format, the whole letter is left justified with a single space and has a double space between paragraphs.

Modified block: The modified block format is also widely used. In this format, the body of the letter and the sender's and receiver's addresses are left justified with a single space. However, for the date and closing, the tab is in the center.

Semi-block: Semi-block is the least preferred format. It is quite similar to modified block format; the only difference is that each paragraph is indented rather than being left justified.

It is always wise to follow the organizational format when writing letters.

Business Letters: Font and Punctuation

The font used in business letters is another important factor. The most widely accepted font is Times New Roman, size 12. However, some people prefer using Arial, size 12.

Use a colon (:) after the salutation and after the close. In numerous situations, open punctuation may be used, in which no punctuation is used after the salutation and closing.

Business Letters Layout

Lists and bullets: These help to sequence your ideas and improve the visual effect of your letter. Bullets help to draw the receiver's attention to crucial ideas and make complex things appear simple. These are beneficial for the receiver to quickly skim the text and retain the vital points of the letter.

Headings and subheadings: The purpose of headings and subheadings is to group different ideas into relevant groups. These provide description and information and play a key role in catching the attention of the receiver, organizing different ideas, and providing a logical connection to ideas.

Three-Stage Formula for Writing

Every message, whether sent as a business letter, in an email, or in a memo, succeeds by following this three-stage formula.

PLAN WRITE FINISH

'Plan' every piece of writing beforehand. Planning includes having the answers to the five Ws (who, what, when, where, and why) and one H (how) question ready.

Write the first draft of your communication.

'Finish' by proofreading and editing the first draft to get the final, refined draft.

Routine Letters and Positive News

While writing routine letters, begin by stating your request in a courteous tone. Ensure you are receiver-centric, concrete, and specific. No personal details are required while making your request. Thereafter, proceed to explaining and justifying your request by providing reader benefits. Put forth the most important and relevant questions first. Don't bundle several topics into one question. Finally, conclude with the request for a call to action after sharing a note of goodwill.

Routine requests may be business orders, requests for information and action, and claims and adjustments. For business orders, begin with making the request, state the order correctly and completely, and share shipping details. For letters requesting information and action, begin by giving the reason why you are writing, explain your request in detail, and ask for a specific action. For claims and adjustments, start by describing the problem, supporting your claims, and politely and tactfully requesting an action. Avoid accusations and act with understanding, along with providing alternatives.

Writing Replies to Routine Messages and Positive News

While replying to routine messages and positive news, provide all information, address every question, and close while promoting goodwill. In this case, the direct strategy may be applied, which consists of the main idea, relevant details, and a polite close.

Writing Bad-News Messages

The process to be followed in writing bad-news messages is to convey the message beginning with the reason(s), share a goodwill note, and close after you promote an overall good impression for the organization.

The direct approach to delivering bad news includes giving the bad news followed by a reason or reasons and ending on a positive note, while the indirect approach begins with a buffer followed by reasons and bad news and ends on a positive note.

If you plan to begin with a buffer, be sincere, polite, neutral, crisp, and brief. While providing the reason(s) supporting your refusal or rejection, give appropriate details and provide logic. Avoid apologizing and using negative words or phrases. Deliver the bad news while focusing on the positive and staying away from ambiguity. Close confidently and with sincerity.

Direct Approach	Indirect Approach
Open with main point (bad news)	Open with neutral buffer
Body supports information/ provides reason/s	Body explains/gives reason and negative news
Close with positive statement	Close with goodwill

Some formats are given as follows.

Claim about a Faulty Printing System

Dear Mr Shaw,

The new automated printing system you sent us (Invoice #11112) has broken, thus considerably slowing the printing process in our company showroom.

Although the printing system worked well after installation, due to a power failure because of bad weather, problems emerged with it when we started printing copies of a large document. After a few 100 pages, there was a smoke in the sheet feeder and it stopped working.

The product is under warranty period of twelve months provided by your company. We are shipping the sheet feeder to you by Express Couriers. We would like it either repaired or replaced. Your early action will help our showroom to return to normal soon.

Sincerely,
Ruby Roy

Positive Response to the Previous Claim

Dear Ms Roy,

The sheet feeder of your printing system is now working and should arrive in Mangalore by courier in two days. Please get it installed by your technician to protect the warranty.

You reported that the sheet feeder smoked before the printing system stopped working. We have checked the sheet feeder and found that due to a cross-connection, it got overheated and melted, and it smoked as per the design to protect the printing system and your staff from electrical shock.

You might be interested in our new scanning system made for bulk scanning, which is compatible with your printing system. The enclosed brochure has the details. We will be glad to discuss in case you need more details.

Sincerely,
Ronny Shaw

Negative Response to the Previous Claim

Dear Ms Roy,

Tresma Co. does guarantee its printing systems for twelve months in normal operation under normal situations.

Our technicians examined the returned sheet feeder of your printing system and found that the sheet feeder smoked due to the short circuit because of the power failure. While the printing system has been designed to face such resistance, our manual clearly indicates the backup requirement, which was apparently missing in your case.

In view of this, we are unable to process your request for a repair or a replacement.

You might be interested in buying a new sheet feeder with more features and compatible with your existing printing system, power failure adaptable with twelve months' warranty. We would like to offer it at a flat discount of 15 per cent for you are our existing client. The enclosed brochure has the details. We will be glad to discuss in case you need more details.

Sincerely,
Ronny Shaw

Persuasive Letter (Job Application)

Dear Ms Harrison,

Pysum's is about to open its fifth store in its food chain in Hyderabad, and you are looking for more staff of part-time employees to assist your full-time employees. I believe I have the required background and motivation to become one of your most productive part-time employees.

Pursuing hotel management from a ranked university, I am currently focusing on food management courses. I could apply my learning over the next one year to my floor manager work at Pysum's. The job references listed on the enclosed résumé will attest that I am very energetic about my work. Another reason I think I would make a good part-time employee for you is that I am very keen on pursuing a career at Pysum's after graduation. I would see this coming year as a period to prove my worth, and you would have the year to decide whether or not I am a suitable fit for your food chain.

It would be a great opportunity if we could connect to discuss my suitability for the position.

Sincerely,
Aneeta Blesna

Information Letter

Dear Ms Varghese,

I write to update you of our latest pricing model effective 10 July 2021. On 10 January, we are transferring from a half-yearly billing period to a quarterly billing period, and I share some significant information that could affect your company.

Following detailed examination and obtaining feedback from our clients, it has been concluded that the majority clients have a special preference to a quarterly billing cycle rather than a half-yearly. Keeping your interest in mind, we are determined to offer this advantage, which will be effectual from 10 July 2021.

Through this communication, we keep you updated of the coming alterations. We appreciate your association with us.

Sincerely,
Johny Paulson

Letter after the First Meeting

Dear Ms Banerjee,

It was indeed very pleasant to meet you at the trade fair yesterday. As discussed, I believe that the durability of XYZ footstep count bands assembled by my company PQR Ltd can greatly make a combo pack with the ABC heartbeat bands that your company BBV Ltd produces and sells. I would like to visit your office with two of my team members and discuss the best option for our collaboration.

Our meeting will give an opportunity to understand and assess the needs of our joint venture in future. We are available to meet any time over the next week. Please share your convenient time for us to meet.

Sincerely,
Jack Thomas

Report Writing

What Is a Report?

Isn't report writing an integral part of your work? A report is prepared to provide information with a particular purpose to a specific audience. A report is a structured way of presenting information and evidence which have been analysed and employed to an issue. A report facilitates decision-making. You have a report brief so that you are able to write a report. The report brief outlines the objective, audience and issue that your report must cater to, along with the required format.

Objectives of a Report

- To provide information about an organization's plans, progress, issues, etc.
- To suggest a particular action
- To present facts to enable decision-making
- To justify a course of action

What Constitutes a High-Quality Report?

For your report to be of the best quality, it should:

- Be concise and concrete
- Be factual
- Have proper use of visuals (tables and graphs)
- Be highly structured
- Be numbered with headings and subheadings
- Follow an executive summary
- Provide recommendations and conclusions

Structure of a Report

Most organizations follow their own guidelines for a report. The basic features of a report, however, are more or less similar.

- Cover
- Title Page
- Acknowledgements
- Table of Contents
- Executive Summary
- Introduction
- Discussion
- Conclusion
- Recommendations
- Appendix
- References
- Bibliography
- Glossary

Title Page
The title page consists of

- Heading
- Name and affiliation of the report writer
- Date
- For whom the report is written

Example of a title page is given as follows:

Identification of Market Potential and Entry Strategy
for Environment-Friendly Cloth Bags

Submitted to
Mr Ritesh Sen
Chief Executive Officer

By
Sneha Pant
Marketing Manager

JJH Packaging Ltd
Surat, Gujarat
16 September 2022

Terms of Reference

Terms of reference include a short description of the audience, purpose, scope and methods of the report. It may be the subtitle or a separate paragraph.

Acknowledgements

This part includes acknowledging and expressing gratitude to each person and organization associated with the report by providing information, advice or assistance.

Table of Contents

The table of contents identifies the topics and their page numbers. It also indicates the order in which the topics are worded and laid in the report.

Sample Table of Contents

Executive Summary

The executive summary is a brief account of the report. It includes the key features of the report: background, problem, major details, conclusion(s), and recommendation(s).

Sample executive summary:

This report was written to figure out why the number of Tomateena Sauce sales has gone down since 2017, when they were at their highest, and to come up with ways to boost them.

The study draws attention to the fact that in 2017, the market share of Tomateena Sauce was 43 per cent. The shares of the other major players, such as Saggie and Winrise, were 21 per cent and 17 per cent, respectively. The size of the sauce market then was $52 million. During the coming two years, Tomateena Sauce did maintain its market share, but the sales volume in the entire market decreased to $32 million. More probes make known that this market decline was due to a rise in health awareness among customers who regard the sugar ingredients in sauce as adverse. In addition, since the second half of 2018, more rivals producing sauce have emerged in the market with their sauces without sugar. These products claimed to give health benefits along with taste to the customers. Due to these factors, the sales volume of Tomateena Sauce decreased.

Tomateena Sugar-free Sauce is the latest sauce range offered by the R&D department of Tomateena Sauce. The report assesses this range and concludes that it is the right response of Tomateena Sauce to encounter the challenge presented by the market and will gratify the new demand from the customers because it is sugar-free and endorsed by prominent health professionals and dieticians. According to 96 per cent of the 3000 subjects who tasted the product recently, it has the same taste as the original Tomateena Sauce.

It is recommended that

- Tomateena Sauce takes fast action to launch and promote sugar-free sauce with its existing product range.
- Sugar-free sauce assumes a healthy appearance.
- Sugar-free sauce is available in all department stores and small grocery shops, as well as in food marts.

Introduction

The introduction includes the current business scenario of the organization, the background, which includes the purpose for the report, the research problem, the scope of the study and the theoretical framework for the study, including research methods, data grouping and data analysis. The results are to be presented as findings.

Discussion

This is the main body of the report. It discusses findings and analysis. The evidence is discussed in this part. If the discussion part is very lengthy, you might divide it into headings and subheadings, depending on the length. Sequence the discussion logically for better understanding.

Conclusion

The conclusion provides the results and overall significance of the study. The key points may be reminded along with answers to issues raised at the beginning, but no new information is to be given in the conclusion part.

Recommendations

These are the points for a call to action. They demonstrate how the conclusions should be implemented. Recommendations are specific proposals. A report is incomplete without recommendations. Just like conclusions are drawn from discussion, recommendations are derived from conclusions.

Appendices

Everything that you used during the study but did not present in any other part of the report is presented under the appendices. These include tables, graphs and survey questionnaires. The location in the appendix should be quoted in the body of the report. For example, in order to evaluate the acceptance of the proposed change, a questionnaire (Appendix 3) was administered to seventy candidates. The results (Appendix 4) signify that the change is welcomed by the majority of the candidates.

Bibliography

The bibliography lists all published and unpublished sources of information you used in the report. All documents you referred to—past years' reports, periodicals, articles, books, etc.—are to be included in the bibliography. There are various styles of writing the bibliography, and the most standard ones are by the Modern Language Association or the American Psychological Association.

Glossary

It provides an alphabetical list of technical terms, describing each term briefly and clearly. Abbreviations, acronyms, and standard units used in the report can be included in the glossary.

In a Nutshell

Effective writing is the result of clarity of thought. The clearer your thoughts are, the more effective your writing is! Think clearly, plan accordingly, create the first draft, and finalize your business writing with diligent editing.

5

In Good Voice

People who know what they're talking about, don't need PowerPoint.

—**Steve Jobs**

A very important client is visiting your organization to close a crucial deal. Before signing the documents, the client expects to have a final look at the project details. Your manager had anticipated this and advised you to be ready with the project presentation. You realize the seriousness of the situation very well, but what is this? Do you have some butterflies in your stomach? Are you extremely nervous before the presentation?

Very often, our work requires us to provide opinions, share ideas, have dialogues and conversations, give Ted Talks, etc. In a way, it requires us to make a presentation, at times formal and other times informal. Ideal presentations are all about connecting the right dots and are a combination of a description and a story. A description has information, while a story has engagement and connection. Presentations are done for varied purposes.

Project report presentation: Share the information document with the audience to avoid unnecessary questions. Present the findings only.

Financial report: Now, this is where you can use data, facts, figures, numbers, etc. But don't let it be dry (data alone). Weave a narrative to make it appealing. Present the findings with images and visuals.

Product/service launch: Here is an opportunity to demonstrate your storytelling skills. Mention features and specifications, but concentrate more on the value your product or service will offer.

Ted talks: A creative story web will do the task. Make situations and emotions run through your story to keep the audience hooked on your message.

Motivational or pep talks: Converse with and interact with the employees. Let it be a dialogue. Have an open house kind of environment.

Formal talks: Choose your subject matter relevant to the event or occasion. Ensure a clear storyline to maintain audience interest.

Prepare, Prepare, Prepare!

Preparation is the key to an effective presentation. The subject matter is of the utmost importance. Without a cake, there can be no icing! The subject matter is your cake, and the way you deliver it is the icing you apply to decorate the already-delicious cake. These two complement each other. Without proper delivery, the subject matter, however important it is, might not be as interesting as it would be with proper delivery. Similarly, who wants only icing on a bad cake? Just an effective drug very cannot do magic and change the fate of a bad substance or subject matter. In fact, the basis of every presentation is your well-thought-out message. Clarity of the subject matter adds to your confidence as well. Once that is in place, you need to think about the delivery. In addition to the why (objective), what (subject matter/cake), and how (delivery/icing), there are numerous other things that are to be looked into, like the venue, timing, duration of the presentation or talk, audience and visual aids.

Why (Objective)

You are asked to speak to undergraduate students, highlighting the importance of mental health. Your talk might be scheduled as one of the guest talks during a health week celebration at the college, and the students might have felt the need to know more about it. Now you are aware that your talk has to be not only engaging and woven into a story, but also carry a message with a touch of humour in between. You need to cater to the expectations of the audience and the organizers.

Before any presentation with any audience, ask what the objective of the presentation is. Simply put, why are you required to be present? The answer to this question will facilitate you in structuring your presentation and tailoring it to meet the objective or objectives.

What (Subject Matter/Cake)

The 'what' follows the 'why'. The subject matter is derived from the objective of the talk or presentation.

The subject may be given to you by the organizers, you might be presenting the details of a completed project before your colleagues, you might be asked to talk about your area of expertise, and so on.

Venue

Try to get as much information as possible, well in advance, about the venue of your talk or presentation. This is one thing that helps you manage the nervousness associated with presentations. If possible, visit the venue some day before your talk or, at least, some time before your talk. Familiarity with the venue eases handling things that might go out of control on the day of the presentation. If visiting is difficult, get the following information:

- Size of the room
- Seating plan
- Required equipment such as a microphone, laptop and projector.
- Light in the room

Even when you are presenting in the boardroom of your office, which you are familiar with, do reach a bit earlier than the others to feel the comfort of reaching before them.

Timing

Most of the time, you may not have the liberty to choose the timing of your presentation. Morning, of course, is the most acceptable time for a presentation because people are energetic. Tea breaks ensure people don't start looking at the clock for a lunch break. If given a choice, choose the morning hours for your session.

Afternoons are ideally avoided because, after lunch, people are inactive and sluggish. However, if you are to present after lunch, employ strategies to involve the audience. It may be a discussion, an activity, or an exercise, depending on the nature of your presentation or talk. Remember, your slides might lull them to sleep.

Evening time is fine for audience involvement as long as it is within regular hours, but there are issues, especially if it gets prolonged after office hours. The audience might be physically present if required, but attention will be lost the moment you extend your talk.

If you are prepared in advance, timing will not be a challenge. Slightly modify the delivery and organize your presentation based on the timing.

Duration

Knowing the duration of your talk helps plan it accordingly. Clarify if it is inclusive of a question-and-answer session. While doing a business presentation, even if it is for a familiar audience (your colleagues), ensure your presentation is succinct and engaging. A thirty- to forty-minute main session followed by a ten- to fifteen-minute Q&A is acceptable for most people. You are presenting with an objective, so make an attempt to not let the audience feel you wasted their time. If it is an invited talk, check the order in which you are presenting and wait with cool nerves for your turn. At times, being the last person to speak could be catastrophic; nonetheless, you need to know how to still give your best and keep the audience glued until you finish.

Audience

Understanding the audience will enable you to customize your presentation. In the case of invited talks, find out the size of the audience, age group and educational backgrounds, find out the size of the audience, age group and educational background. By giving them due consideration, you will be able to model your talk according to their understanding, and they will be able to better relate to you.

Visual Aids

Visual aids complement your presentations and talks. They assist in engaging the audience and support your point with pictures, sounds and videos. And you know that what we see leaves a more lasting effect than what we just hear or listen to. Visual aids include, but are not limited to, PowerPoint slides, handouts, flip charts and props. If used with care, visual aids add effect to the presentation and engage the audience. But remember, don't let them replace you! Also, do not let its improper use wreck your presentation. Use visual aids only if needed. In case you need technical support for your visual aids, ensure there is such an arrangement much before the presentation.

Organizing and Writing the Presentation

Use the magic of the number three, since it has been found that people retain three points or key messages for a longer time than four or more. Ensure your talk is structured at least in three sections.

Introduction

Organizing: Begin with the subject and significant features of your presentation. Draw your audience's attention with a clear and specific rationale for your presentation. Set expectations regarding questions, whether you would appreciate those at the end of your presentation or you would be fine taking questions while you are presenting.

Writing: Write down the flow of your presentation so that the audience knows beforehand what is to follow.

Main Body

Organizing: Expand on the significant features with evidence. Keep the length short and the elements crisp. It's better to have 2–3 key points for a fifteen-minute presentation, 4–6 for a half-hour presentation, and 6–8 for a forty-five-minute presentation. Have a logical sequence of the points and elaborate them using CRE (claim, reason, and evidence, discussed in Chapter 6).

Writing: Have just two or three ideas to share. Avoid bullet points; they are outdated now; rather, choose bubbles. If there are more than three, choose the ones you want your audience to retain longer and present only those.

For example, while presenting about the new marketing avenues, you may use the following figure:

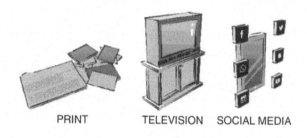

PRINT   TELEVISION   SOCIAL MEDIA

Edit your presentation for language, choice of words, grammar and spelling. Use short sentences. Use jargon only when you are sure the audience is familiar with it. The audience will listen to your presentation, so keep it simple. Maintain a logical sequence while presenting. Use stories, audience activities (based on the presentation type), short videos, a picture, or a flashcard in this section of your presentation.

Conclusion

Organizing: Summarize the significant features of your presentation. To avoid confusion, choose words that show that you are concluding. Open the session for the audience to ask questions.

Writing: Jot down the wrap-up followed by the indication of closure with a 'thank you' and/or 'questions, please'.

Choosing the Presentation Method

The method of presentation will vary according to several factors.

Event: Your approach will obviously vary when you are speaking to an audience of more than 100 people at a conference as opposed to a group of five people in a meeting room.

Audience and topic: For an informal or semi-formal talk for a small group, you might use a handout with your thoughts bulleted and discuss them through, while for a bigger group, you might use slides or other methods of presentation.

Available resources: The available resources, at times, determine the method of your presentation. In the absence of a projector, you are left with no choice but to explore other options without slides.

Experience and expertise: The method of presentation varies with your experience and expertise. The more experienced you become at presenting and the more expertise you have in the topic of your presentation, the more likely it is for you to use fewer or no slides and present with your notes or even without those.

How (Delivery/Icing)

This involves a number of things, right from your body language to your eye contact to your voice modulation, including pauses, word and sentence stress, as well as pronunciation.

Body Language

If you can help it, don't talk from behind the podium. Most of your body won't be visible, making it hard for the audience to understand what you're saying with your body. Being stationed at one place or moving around makes a difference. If the podium cannot be done away with, use it only for changing the slides and move during the presentation.

How you move matters a lot. Keep away from pacing to and fro and back and forth repeatedly. Ensure that the audience does not predict your next movement. They should not feel like spectators at a tennis match, moving their necks from one end to the other to keep pace with your movement. Decide on a particular zone that you will use for moving without obstructing the presentation. Move a few steps from where you are to your left, stay there for a few seconds, and, gradually, come to the center while presenting. Pause for a few moments there, and then move to the other side.

Pauses in movement give you time to maintain that much-needed eye contact with the audience. Avoid gazing at or staring at one member of the audience. Use a Z or N in your mind to appear, maintaining eye contact with most people in the audience. Refrain from talking to the ceiling or to the floor.

Maintain a relaxed and tall posture with open arms while presenting. Don't rest on the podium or shift your weight from one foot to the other. Some movement after regular intervals helps keep away from weight shifting.

Ensure that your gestures are balanced—neither absent nor too many. Use energy and power gestures during Ted talks and motivational talks; avoid using those during business presentations, keynote speeches and other formal talks. Avoid putting your hands in your pockets or behind you.

You don't gesture all the time while presenting, right? Do you wonder at times what to do with your hands while you are not gesturing? What do you do after some time of cycling? You stop and put the bike on a rest or stand. Similarly, when you are not gesturing, use a handstand.

In this figure, you can see that the hands are in front, below your chin and above your belly. A little above will cover your face, and a little below may not appear professional. Fingers of both hands touching without clasping each other.

Avoid fiddling with the pen, the watch, or your hair.

Paralanguage

The content of the presentation, as well as the speaker's body language and other non-verbal cues, are what keep the audience interested. Paralanguage includes volume and pitch variation, voice modulation, speed of speaking, word or sentence stress and pauses.

Use words easily understood by the audience, speak neither too fast nor too slow, adjust your volume to the size of the venue and the distance from the audience, stress the right words or sentences to add emphasis, use rising and falling tones to involve the audience, take proper pauses for creating an effect, and avoid jargons. Your voice shows your sincerity and enthusiasm.

Butterflies in the Stomach?

It's okay to have them as long as they help you excel. Presentation nervousness is natural and very common! Even experienced lecturers, seasoned speakers, and the best orators feel nervous, despite years of presentation experience. In fact, in every professional meeting, people in the public eye, such as politicians, celebrities, and media people, feel nervous. Our nervousness erupts in the form of butterflies (an uneasy feeling) in the stomach, sweaty palms, a parched throat, and out of words and thoughts. But you need not worry! Try to control your nerves with mindfulness and other techniques. Using these techniques will pump your hormones, resulting in an enthusiastic presentation or talk.

The first key to overcoming a presentation is to 'be well prepared!' Have a good sleep the night before the presentation.

Tips to Win Presentation Nervousness

Before the Presentation	During the Presentation
Take deep breaths	Smile
Sip warm water	Pause
Do a mindfulness exercise for positivity	Be in the moment (clear the cobwebs)
Do a stretching exercise (standing/sitting)	Move naturally and occasionally
Visualize	Connect with the audience

Q&A

The session that is often dreaded is the Q&A. Learning to handle questions effectively makes it easy to navigate through the session. Tell yourself that people are honestly interested in getting the answers; they are not asking questions to bother you. Avoiding questions is a strict no-no.

Listen to the question actively and paraphrase for better understanding.

Take charge of the situation.

Don't give wrong answers or bluff; people are sensible enough to see through it.

Be assertive! If the question is inciting, don't get caught off guard; don't panic. Instead, relax, take a pause, paraphrase, and give an honest response.

If it is an unrelated question, say, 'Let's discuss this offline' or 'That's interesting!' Let us exchange contacts and discuss this some other time.

If you haven't anticipated the question and are unprepared for it, say, 'Please allow me to reply with this response in a day's time' or 'I would surely contemplate this question and revert to you by tomorrow.'

Relax! You are not a know-all. Don't show off. If you don't know an answer, say, 'May I get back to you?'

Storytelling

In a small village lived a young girl with her parents.

Stories have been an integral part of our upbringing and have been with us since time immemorial. They have shaped our behaviors and conduct, guided us, motivated us, and taught us lessons. We remember most of the stories we listened to in our childhood and share them with our young generations. No matter what our age is, we get engrossed in stories so intensely. These are the very reasons we can bring storytelling into presentations. Starting a presentation with a story is a good idea, but what if our entire presentation is in the form of a story? We want our receivers to respond to us and remember the key takeaways from our presentation, and stories have more power to achieve both of these objectives than the bullet points on our slides.

Stories arouse emotions and engage the audience. The dry facts, figures, and information, when woven into the fabric of a story, give them meaning and add life.

What is the Nucleus of Your Story?

Character

Living beings have stories; non-living things don't. Focus on the character instead of the product or service. Instead of focusing on what the new HR policy (a non-living thing) states, focus on how it works for the employees (living beings). Focus more on the children (living beings) who will consume your company's biscuits than on the ingredients in the biscuits (non-living things).

Climax

A story with a change in the situation in the climax is always appreciated. It should be a journey from what should have been to what is your contribution towards it. For instance, did the pollution in the environment motivate you to come up with the idea of green fuel? Did the situation of employees with children lead you to introduce paternity leave in your organization?

Good stories are:

- Not more than 2–3 minutes long
- Honest
- Woven into the context, not forced
- Tailored according to the audience, topic and occasion
- Remembered for a long time
- Visual portrayals

Sources of stories

Stories largely emerge from your or others' experiences, from literature, newspapers, television, movies, history and mythology. Adapt stories, give the existing ones a creative twist, and add your touch to them.

The Art of Storytelling

Having a good story is not enough. It has to be narrated with impact. Mix emotions and use non-verbal cues to make it more effective. Your facial expressions, gestures, movements, posture, eye contact and voice modulation together lead to a powerful story, which your audience can relate to.

Eternal Storytelling Techniques

These five storytelling techniques carry the 'aha' factor and mostly work wonders.

1. **Monomyth/The Hero's Journey: The monomyth** is also referred to as the hero's journey. This technique is commonly seen in mythology and folktales. It calls for the protagonists to leave their homes and move on a tough journey, from a friendly, known zone to a hostile, unknown zone. After fighting all struggles, they return victorious and wiser for their community.

This technique will facilitate your sharing with your audience the wisdom you gained from your presentation.

2. **Peak:** Peak is somewhat similar to Monomyth in that it can be used to indicate the happenings in the plot of the story. Unlike Monomyth, Peak may not have a cheerful ending. Peak comprises the highs and lows of a journey and reaches the end. It is like a soap opera with a lot of drama culminating in an ending.

3. **Concoction:** Concoction is a technique where stories are interlinked. You have one key story, and you build other stories around it to explain the vital assumption. You begin with the main story

but sandwich a few side stories in between, at the beginning and towards the end of the main story. For example, your main story is about a life of learning. You begin with it. But immediately, you discuss a neighbour's experience, who learned a lesson from a friend. Finally, you get your answer in the form of a life lesson. Here, you find the concoction of the neighbour's experience based on an experience with a friend, which ultimately leads you to a life lesson.

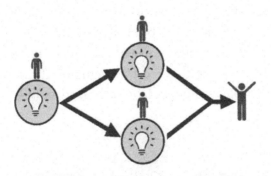

4. **Reality to Hope:** Nancy Duarte calls it Sparklines and indicates that these are the best talks as they transport the audience from the ordinary to the extraordinary. The 'from reality to hope' technique attracts the audience's attention to the issues in their lives, around them, and at their workplaces, after which the speaker takes the audience to the world of hope, inculcating in them the desire to become change drivers.

5. **Fabricated Beginning:** A fabricated beginning is when you start with a known tale, abruptly pause it, and begin afresh with some shock. Such stories can help you talk about a new idea you or your organization came up with or a creative idea you want to share that led to a remake. It talks about rising like a phoenix from ashes, from failures.

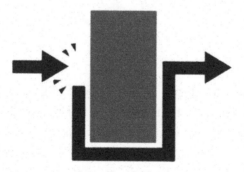

6. **Pearl String:** The pearl string technique embeds different stories leading to a central theme. You may use your different experiences or weave the narratives of different people you may have

come across toward the key message. Ensure you give signals about how these are connected with each other. Such a weaving of experiences adds credibility to your message. Connect the different experiences into a single narrative around your message.

TED Talks

TED Talks give you an opportunity to speak your heart, and if you are able to do it by creating an enchanting story, nothing can beat it! These are honest expressions that take the audience on a journey with you, live your narrative with you, laugh with you, be sad with you, be thrilled with you, and get afraid with you.

1. **Soak the audience:** You succeed at storytelling when your audience remembers your story for a long time. Excellent TED Talks are those that cater

to all the senses of the receivers. Paint your story with images, fragrances, visuals and sounds. Give the audience space to visualize your story as a film. The rule is to keep it short and crisp.

2. **Give your story a personal touch.** A personal touch brings credibility to your story. Be the protagonist of the story. Follow one of the techniques shared above and go ahead.

3. **Live characters:** Characters form the core of any talk. Empower your characters to make people laugh, be happy, and be curious. Describe them in detail for people to remember, whether it is how they look, how they walk, or what their likes and dislikes are.

4. **Demonstrations and visuals:** Let the audience transcend into the story itself through demonstrations and visuals. Weave minor details into the narration to take the audience through the lives of the characters as their own.

5. **WOW factor:** Let there be a WOW factor to your talk, such that it will be remembered whenever your talk is mentioned.

6. **What's in it for me?** TED Talks generally carry a message, and that too a positive one. Squeeze it into a catchy phrase that becomes your signature style.

Feedback

How many times do we receive feedback or have the itch to give it? Feedback is almost inescapable and an important aspect of every organization. Workplaces that ensure a frequent and free flow of feedback flourish and thrive. In addition to boosting morale, feedback is an opportunity to understand strengths and areas for improvement in our work, behaviour and personality. Giving feedback is a skill, since it is not just about conveying information but communication that begins with listening. Whether positive or negative, constructive feedback produces a desirable result. Feedback creates a healthy workplace, enhances engagement, increases productivity, and brings magical effects to communication and team spirit.

Giving feedback requires skill. Let us look at how to give constructive feedback along with a few instances.

Focusing on what went right: This is very useful when giving negative feedback. Start with the discussion of the project, asking, 'What is your view?' Continue critically examining the project while sharing the feedback. Criticism will not be taken personally when it is given objectively. Try to make the person understand what went wrong instead of pointing out the wrongs done.

Being specific: Generalizing statements such as 'You're not sincere' or 'You are lackadaisical' is an invitation to trouble. An attack on character only causes ill feelings. Do your homework on the particular behaviors and actions of the people you are giving feedback to. Talk about what was done rather than the intention behind it; discuss how those behaviors and actions are affecting you, the team and the organization as a whole; clearly explain your expectations regarding change in those behaviors and actions. Refrain from sentences starting with 'You never . . .' or 'You always . . .'

In place of 'good job', say, 'You did a good presentation.'

Using positive statements: Feedback given on a positive note results in improvement and is not taken defensively.

Instead of: 'You wrote a terrible report.'

Say: 'The report has some issues that are not in line with the company's expectations. Could you please revisit it?'

in place of: 'Your file is unclear and full of unnecessary details.'

Say: 'This file will be more useful if it is made concise and clear.'

Practical advice: It is very important to give practical advice while giving negative feedback. Criticism without suggestions for improvement does not add value. The purpose of your feedback is to improve the performance.

In place of: 'Why were you looking down while talking to the client?'

Say: 'Your presentation was factual and clear. Try looking at the client while speaking; it will be more appealing. I can help you with some tips.'

Making it a habit: For feedback to really work, you should make it a habit and not wait for the annual feedback season, when you apprise the employees of their progress. This is all the more necessary when one of them has not completed a task as required. Timely feedback helps the employee not repeat the same mistake.

In place of: 'I will discuss this project report in our next personal meeting.'

Say: 'I would like to discuss with you the project report you just completed. When may we meet for a ten-minute discussion in the next week?'

Eye-to-eye communication: Let feedback be a very personal and special affair. Don't make it impersonal by giving it over email or message. Eye-to-eye communication gives the employee a chance to seek answers to questions, clarify, and give honest feedback.

In place of: 'I will send you a message regarding your task.'

Say: 'Let's discuss your task over a cup of coffee when you are free this week.'

Lending your ear: Have a dialogue during the feedback session where you also listen and not just speak.

Maybe the expectations were not clear, or maybe there were misunderstandings due to which something went wrong. Feedback is useful if taken in the right spirit, and for that to happen, you need to give the receivers a chance to share their side of the story.

Videoconferencing

In this era of the new normal in the form of remote working, videoconferencing is a boon. Videoconferencing is used to organize a conference between two or more attendees located at various places through audio and video transmission computer networks. It is similar to video calling. This mode of communication enhances productivity in organizations and quickens decision-making in spite of the different locations of the attendees. Due to its viability and the feature of saving time and effort, videoconferencing has become a significant way for organizations to connect with internal and external stakeholders with equal ease. However, as human beings, we are aware that if such interactions are to be impactful, we need to develop specific communication skills.

Communicating Powerfully During Videoconferencing

Videoconferencing will lose its essence if it is ineffective and unproductive. It is all the more important to communicate sensibly and sensitively during videoconferencing, since there could be easy misunderstandings with less or no chance of correction or clarification as in the case of face-to-face conversations. Conveying the right impression through your body language and paralanguage is vital in the case of videoconferencing. A few pointers may facilitate smooth conversations virtually.

Getting Ready

Just like you get ready for an in-person meeting, get ready for the online meeting as well. Certain things, along with your getting ready, will make the process smooth.

- Ensure proper lighting in the room. The source of light must be in front of you and behind the camera of your device.
- Sit in a chair with your device on a table or any stable surface.
- It is ideal to do the online meeting in a silent, closed room with no disturbance from the surrounding sounds.
- Ensure your microphone and speaker are of good quality.
- Wear professional attire and have a pleasant appearance.

- Make sure your face covers only one-third of the screen.
- Prefer neutral shades for virtual backgrounds.

Facial Expressions

The key to being good at online meetings is to treat them as if they were face-to-face. Even while you are listening, ensure your face doesn't look dull. Be energetic, listen with a slight raise of the eyebrows, and nod when required; listening with a tilted head shows interest.

Body Posture

Sit with an open body posture and a slight lean. Sit comfortably, but don't appear slack. Good posture makes you appear energetic and healthy. In a video meeting, your body from your waist up is only visible, but remember that it does not permit you to move your legs because, ultimately, it will show on your posture and divert the audience. So sit still. Also, sit up straight because then your voice modulation will be better understood. A slight lean forward conveys your interest.

Gestures

Gestures should be tailored according to the number of audience members. If it is one or two, go for small gestures. However, with a large number, you may use big gestures. Use strong gestures, but don't overdo them. Keep away from excessive gestures. Avoid touching your eyebrows or nose while discussing. When not gesturing, place your hands on the arm rest or on the table beside the device. Refrain from crossing your arms, which is considered a closed body posture.

Eye Contact

Eye contact is very important in online meetings. Avoid looking at yourself. Look at the lens; that's where the audience is. If there is an option, close the self-view and interact with the audience.

Paralanguage

Pay special attention to paralanguage during online meetings. Your voice is a powerful tool to show that you are enthusiastic. Pronounce the words correctly and have a balanced speaking speed—neither too fast nor too slow. The warmth and vigour in your voice keep the online meetings full of liveliness. Take relevant pauses, but not very long.

Smile

The best way to develop and maintain rapport with your recipient is to smile. For instance, whether it is a first-time client or a long-time client, look into the camera for a moment, smile, and greet before the meeting begins. This gives a cordial beginning to a trustful relationship. A smile also helps ease tensions and conflicts and leads to positive results. A note of caution: don't smile frequently and don't fake it. It might be misread and adversely affect your credibility. Conversely, not smiling at all makes you appear unfriendly.

Words Are Valuable Too!

Pay absolute attention to the choice of words in online meetings. Think before you speak rather than apologizing later; however, inadvertent errors could be apologized for. Use words with a single meaning. Avoid jargon and clichés.

Whether we like it or not, videoconferencing and online meetings are here to stay for a long time. It is better to be equipped while taking care of small details, including the choice of words and diction along with body language and paralanguage.

In a Nutshell

Whether it is presenting before an audience using storytelling techniques, sharing feedback at the workplace, or videoconferencing, you need to be receiver-centric. Command over the content, audience analysis, a unique style, the right choice of words combined with perfect delivery, in terms of non-verbal communication and audience engagement are promising elements that will lead you to success at all kinds of presentations, including videoconferencing.

6

Connecting across Cultures

The essence of cross-cultural communication has more to do with releasing responses than with sending messages. It is more important to release the right response than to send the right message.

—Edward T. Hall

Culture is the lens through which we look at the world around us. The word 'culture' comes from a French term that originates from the Latin *colere*, which means to cultivate the earth, to grow and nurture. Culture is the shared behaviour and beliefs of a specific social, ethnic, or age group. It encompasses language, food habits, religion, music, arts, customs, traditions and law. It is a way of life.

The elements of culture, as identified by research, include symbols (Lawley, 1994), languages (Swartz,

1997), values (Griswold, 2004), beliefs (Swidler, 1986), identity (Giddens, 2005) and norms (Corchia, 2010). Culture distinguishes one person from another, one society from another, and one organization from another. We follow culture at various stages: the culture we are brought up in (family and surroundings), national culture (country), work culture and cultures other than these (international).

Since the world is becoming more like a small town, it is more important than ever to learn about other cultures. Today, many of us work with people from foreign lands, either in their country or ours.

Cultural sensitivity is needed not just to win business deals but also to win the hearts of our counterparts so that our deals are not one-time affairs but enduring in essence. Moreover, knowing each other's culture facilitates communication like never before.

Before doing business or working in a different country, it has become common to go to a cultural training. It is not just language that makes cross-cultural training effective. The training workshops should, additionally, consist of sensitization sessions about society and culture as a whole for being sustainable.

Enhancing Cross-Cultural Communication

Cross-cultural communication is how people with different nationalities, ethnicities, work styles, cultures, etc., talk to each other. In other words, it refers to agreed meanings expressed through language and non-verbal behaviour. The major focus of cross-cultural communication is to avoid misunderstandings, which ultimately lead to conflicts and problems between people and groups.

Eminent scholars have put forth a variety of models and frameworks for understanding cross-cultural communication. One such model offered by anthropologist Edward Hall in the 1950s is where he talks about high- and low-context cultures.

Edward Hall's Model

Here's an exchange between an Indian and a Canadian:

I: Hope I have made myself clear on all the points we discussed just now. (Speaker owns the responsibility for understanding.)

C: Yes, and did you follow what I shared with you? (Speaker places the responsibility for understanding on receiver.)

I: What are your views on the project, finally? (scope for open response)

C: Do you accept our pricing policy? (requires yes or no as a response)

I: It is a little difficult to accept. (Indirect way of saying, 'No')

C: We can't approve the deal further. (A direct 'No')

High-Context Cultures	Low-Context Cultures
Indirect and verbose communication	Direct and concise communication
Preference for face-to-face communication	Preference for communication over electronic technology
Enduring relationships	Short-lived relationships
More reliant on context	Less reliant on context
Agreements founded on trust (spoken)	Agreements by legal contract (written)
Clear difference between in-group and out-group	Indistinct difference between in-group and out-group
Deep-rooted cultural patterns, gradual change	Superficial cultural patterns, rapid change
Negotiations sluggish and ritualistic	Negotiations quick and efficient
Tends to use more 'feeling' in expressions	Tends to use 'logic' to present ideas
Credibility through relationships	Credibility through expertise and performance
No business without friendship	Business before friendship
Learning and problem-solving in groups	Learning and problem solving individually

Few examples: India, China, Korea, France, Saudi Arabia, Africa	Few examples: Canada, the US, Sweden, Germany, Norway, Denmark

Having discussed the high and low context cultures, it would be wrong to believe in extremes. Cultures and circumstances have their own highs and lows. We use high- and low-context communication depending upon the situation and our relationship with the receiver. We all heavily rely on a combination of explicit and implicit meanings based on circumstances.

Edward Hall also proposed the difference in cultures based on their patterns of following time as monochronic and polychronic (discussed in Chapter 3).

A social psychologist, Geert Hofstede, advocated cultural dimensions, which assist us in comprehending the unseen foundations of culture. Hofstede's theory is based on six cultural dimensions: Power Distance (PD), individualism versus collectivism, uncertainty avoidance, masculinity versus femininity, long-term versus short-term orientation, and indulgence versus restraint.

Power Distance

In this dimension, the most important thing to talk about is how a society deals with differences between people. PD is the level to which people with less power in a society accept and expect that power is not shared fairly.

The moment A reaches his office, his entire team stands up and wishes him a good morning. He nods at them and signals for them to sit and continue their work. In the meetings he convenes, his team members hesitate to speak; they are scared of questioning him, and decisions are taken by him and his in-group.

Here, you find A is an autocratic leader who: exerts power in his behavior; enjoys the privileges that come by way of his position or designation; has a number of people working under his supervision; likes to patronize and give orders; and maintains hierarchy and inequality. These are the characteristics of a society with a high PD index.

The moment B reaches the office, some of her team members, also walking beside her, say hello to her, while others continue working unaware of her arrival, while a few others wave at her when she crosses their workstations. She answers with a smile, a wave and a 'hi'. In the meetings, she has her team members voice their opinions freely; they question her; they know their rights; and decisions are taken in these meetings after seeking everyone's views.

Here, you find B is participative in nature; she treats her team members as colleagues and not as subordinates; she has few people in her team, likes to mingle with the team, and the structure of the organization is flat. These are the characteristics of a society with a low PD index.

In High PD	In Low PD
Authority is perceived as vertical and formal	Authority is perceived as horizontal and informal
People in authority are considered superior	Manager or boss is just a member of the team
Superiors typically show leadership and take initiative	Any member may take initiative
Less likely to question the boss/manager	Likely to question the boss/manager
Ideas are not expressed openly	Ideas are expressed openly
Directness and informality are considered as insulting	Indirectness and formality are considered as pompous and arrogant
People prefer being called by titles and last names	People prefer being called by first names
Few examples: India, Russia, China, Mexico	Few examples: The UK, Germany, the USA

Individualism versus Collectivism

This dimension shows how much a person would rather be alone and independent than live in a close-knit group.

P lives in a city apartment with her spouse and works for a multinational corporation (MNC). Their parents live in another town. She loves to spend time with herself, pampering herself over the weekends by going to spas, shopping, and going to the opera. She confronts her team whenever required. Whatever she says begins with the first-person pronouns 'I' and 'my'. She is working hard on an ambitious project to get an appraisal. I think you have it! P comes from an individualistic culture, which gives more importance to individual goals, career orientation, independence, competition, confrontation and unique opinions.

Q lives in a town in a huge mansion with his family and also works for an MNC. He loves to spend time with his family over the weekends; he takes them to places of worship, tourist attractions, shopping, etc. He generally keeps quiet at work and does not confront, even when it is required. He shares his things and believes in teamwork and harmony. He does his work sincerely and is waiting for him to complete the required number of years to get promoted. Q comes from a collectivistic culture, which gives more importance to group goals, serious discussions, harmony, organization orientation and conforming views.

Individualism	Collectivism
Employer–employee relations are transactional	Employer–employee relations are cordial
Hiring and promotion decisions are based on individual expertise and efficiency	Hiring and promotion decisions are based on hierarchy
The managerial focus is on success, individual competence and performance	The managerial focus is on group performance and team goals

Individualism	Collectivism
Organizations give priority to tasks	Organizations give priority to relations
Organizations reward those standing out of the crowd, employee of the year, etc.	Organizations reward best team player, etc.
Few examples: the USA, Australia, Germany	Few examples: Bangladesh, China, Algeria

Uncertainty Avoidance Index (UAI)

Uncertainty avoidance is a way to measure how well a society can deal with the unknown. It is not the same as avoiding risk.

A takes risks very easily and is very flexible, adjusting, and open towards the opinions, conduct and actions of others. This is an indicator of low UAI.

On the other hand, B, generally, avoids risk, depends on written norms and procedures, plans things well in advance, and exhibits very little tolerance for those with deviant behaviours. B comes from a society with a high UAI.

High Uncertainty Avoidance Cultures	Low Uncertainty Avoidance Cultures
Stability in job	Entrepreneurial
Clarity	Ambiguity
Structured rules	Less structured rules

High Uncertainty Avoidance Cultures	Low Uncertainty Avoidance Cultures
Social norms—strict	Social norms—flexible
Traditional gender roles	Non-conventional gender roles
Projects are planned properly	Projects are looked at from different angles
Timelines are rigid	Timelines are flexible
Less or no readiness to take risks	More readiness to take risks
Few examples: Japan, Germany, Mexico	Few examples: Singapore, Sweden, Denmark

Masculinity versus Femininity

This dimension indicates how societies distribute emotional roles between genders.

A requests that his team lead reduce his work hours to take care of his kids since his spouse is working on a project that demands long working hours. A belongs to the feminine culture, which believes in quality of life, care and team spirit.

B informs his spouse that he will return home only after completing the project, which could lead to an appraisal. He, too, doesn't forget to share what should be on the menu for dinner that night. B belongs to the masculine culture, which gives more importance to achievement, awards and the notion of distinct gender roles.

High Masculine	Low Masculine (Feminine)
Egocentric	Relationship centric
Money and material very significant, preference for higher pay packet	Quality of life and persons around very significant, preference for few work hours
People live to work	People work to live
Economic growth utmost important	Environment conservation utmost important
Matters resolved through might	Matters resolved through discussions
Wide gender wage gap	Narrow gender wage gap
Less women in management	More women in management
Decisions are taken by people in position	Consensus is sought while making decisions
Centralized work	Decentralized work
Few examples: Slovakia, Japan, Hungary	Few examples: Sweden, Norway, Netherlands

Long-Term versus Short-Term Orientation (Confucian Dynamism)

Long-term orientation (high Confucian values) is characterized by a future-oriented approach to life, while short-term orientation (low Confucian values) is largely focused on the past and present.

P has been working for the same company for 10 years and has been steadily moving up in the company. She saves money for the future and is persistent in whatever she does. P belongs to a society that is long-term oriented, where face consideration is common but perceived as a weakness. These societies respect the demands of virtue.

Q has switched five jobs in the last three years and is now looking at becoming an entrepreneur. He wants quick results. Q comes from a society that is short-term oriented, where protection of the face is important. These societies are concerned with possessing the truth.

Long-term Orientation	Short-term Orientation
Relationships based on status	Status not a key matter in relationships
Personal flexibility significant	Personal stubbornness prevails
More stress on 'what' and 'how'	More stress on 'why'
Either something is good, or it is evil	Good or evil depends on situations
Frugal people	Extravagant people
Willingness to compromise	Less willing to compromise
Few examples: China, Hong Kong, Taiwan, Japan	Few examples: Nigeria, Philippines, Canada, the USA

Indulgence versus Restraint

This dimension focuses on how a society perceives enjoying life. S, an extrovert, works five days a week and spends the weekend with her friend on the beachside drinking, eating and dancing. S belongs to an indulgent society. Indulgence symbolizes allowing free satisfaction of basic human desires with regard to enjoying life and being merry. T, an introvert, also works five days a week but has to spend the weekend taking his parents for prayers, shopping and social get-togethers. T belongs to a restrained society. Restraint indicates crushing of basic human desires by controlling those with severe social rules.

Indulgent Societies	Restrained Societies
People feel happy and healthy	People do not feel happy and healthy
Individuals control their own lives	Individuals believe what happens to them is not their doing
Leisure ethic is a must	Work ethic is a must
Members are positive and optimistic	Members are cynical and pessimistic
Less emphasis on moral discipline	More emphasis on moral discipline
Active participation in sports	Less participation in sports
Few examples: Venezuela, Mexico, Puerto Rico	Few examples: Pakistan, Egypt, Ukraine

Key Business Etiquette in Different Countries

Business frontiers are expanding. Good business results from good relationships, and what works at home may not work across borders. If you are planning to go global, you ought to be sensitized to the business etiquette in different countries. Understanding cultures while doing business facilitates making connections, avoiding a state of embarrassment, and making your receivers feel relaxed.

Let's peek into the key business etiquette in some of the cultures.

China

Gifting is considered good in China. Gift with both hands. Chinese will refuse the gift three times, but you should insist they receive it. Behave similarly when they gift you.

Chinese prefer to be dressed conventionally. They dislike physical contact while discussing.

As a sign of respect, let the Chinese leave the boardroom first after the meeting.

Have a working knowledge of Mandarin.

Japan

Gifting is common, and a nicely wrapped gift is appreciated.

Japanese greet with bowing. A handshake is rare, and even if it is required, let the Japanese initiate it.

Japanese get offended by the word 'no'. Traditionally, they respond with 'yes' or 'it is under consideration', even if they disagree, and that is what they expect from you.

Hierarchy is quite important when leading a meeting. Younger and less experienced people are expected to speak less.

Japanese largely rely on non-verbal communication in a business meeting because they believe in harmony and politeness.

People with similar ranks and positions sit across from each other.

France

The French are quite casual with regard to time. They might come late to work, and people in higher positions might stay late in the office.

Do seek an appointment to meet the French. French people do not appreciate surprise visits.

They like to dress formally on all occasions and are very fashion-conscious.

The French love to have lengthy meals. Don't be restless.

They spend a good deal of money on fashion and looks.

Gifting is fine, but business gifting is expected only after a couple of meetings.

Italy

Gifting is not common in Italy. Once you form a close bond with someone, give a delicate and inexpensive gift, not to showcase your money but as a sign of friendship.

Be very outspoken about timelines with Italians. They tend to be casual like the French with regard to following time.

Business relationships in Italy are based on friendship and trust. Gain those before discussing a deal.

Being the fashion hub of Europe, Italians love to wear trendy, stylish attire. Formal clothes are needed only for business meetings. Women, generally, use add-ons like jewellery and cosmetics.

Dark colours are preferred by men, while women prefer subtle ones.

Germany

Germans communicate directly. Be straightforward in your interactions and transactions with Germans.

Business meetings are properly planned and follow a structure, sticking to the agenda.

No jokes are appreciated at work. Be serious at work.

Germans appreciate punctuality. They expect you to respect their time.

Age is respected, and they appreciate you honouring the elderly.

The United Kingdom

The British expect and appreciate common courtesies like 'please', 'thank you', 'pardon' and 'excuse me' in conversations.

They respect their personal space. So, don't get too close.

They are not comfortable maintaining eye contact for a long time.

Strategies to Excel in Cross-Cultural Communication

Listen before you speak. Active listening will build a positive background to your discussion. Irrespective of culture, human beings appreciate being listened to. Listening also helps create a bridge of understanding since it provides you with pointers upon which you may build. Taking turns during conversations strengthens the discussion. After listening to the host, make a point and then wait for a response.

Mind your questions: Be very specific when asking questions while communicating with a person from a different culture. Ask one question at a time, and make it as specific as possible. Instead of asking, 'Are you joining us now or will you follow after some time?' ask, 'Are you joining us now?'

Paraphrase and summarize: While communicating across cultures, paraphrase while listening to ensure you have the correct meaning with sentences beginning with, 'From what you said, I understand that . . .' and summarize while you are sharing information with sentences beginning with, 'In short . . .', so that misunderstandings, if any, may be sorted out instantly.

No to slang and humour: Don't use slang because it's easy to misunderstand and could offend someone. In the same way, try not to use humor because it might not have the effect you want and hurt the conversation instead. Stick to professionalism.

Research, research, research: Learn as much as you can about the culture before you talk to people from that culture. For example, read about the country, business etiquette, words and phrases to avoid, common courtesies, non-verbal behavior, food habits, etc.

Slow down your speech: English might be the window to the world; however, you should avoid speaking at your normal pace. Adjust your speaking speed while being clear and pronouncing words correctly based on how fast your listener can understand you. Use short sentences. Speaking too fast may result in miscommunication, so it's always ideal to go a bit slow with non-native speakers of English. Slowing down too much might appear condescending. On the other hand, if the person is speaking too fast, you may politely ask them to slow down too. Also, make it a habit to speak facing the receiver so that your words are understood in context with the help of your gestures and facial expressions.

In a Nutshell

Effective listening, being aware of the other person's cultural beliefs, avoiding slang, sarcasm and humour, and showing empathy all go a long way towards mastering the art of cross-cultural communication and winning the hearts of people from other countries.

7

The Creative and Persuasive Spark

Creativity is intelligence having fun.
—**Albert Einstein**

Have you felt something missing after reading the first draft of your email, message, or post? Do you find it drab and uninteresting and just a piece of dry writing?

The purpose of writing is to develop a bond with the reader. Even when we read what we receive, we are looking for a conversation rather than a formal note. You want to read something that touches you personally. Still, when you write, you either completely overlook this aspect or, perhaps, find it difficult and lose your voice while drafting. Then you think you need to polish your writing skills. You start accepting, in despair, that you are not creative enough to be creative in your emails.

What comes to mind when you read the word creativity in writing? A poem, a story, a novel, a jingle, a tagline? Have you ever wondered how you can incorporate creativity into your business writing? The purpose of business writing is to inform, and creative writing is the best way to do so. In business writing, creativity is all about using the best tools, which include words, style and channel. Business writing hones creativity and promotes it.

Before you give up, here's the good news! Creativity is not inborn. If you decide to be creative and practice a little, you will be able to add a pinch of that creative spark you often miss in your business writing. Keep reading further!

1. **So many words!** When you start writing, do you settle for the first word that you think of? If yes, understand that the word is a prevalent one. Consider other words that are even simpler than the first but less common. Experiment with sensual words that have emotions in them. This practice helps add a creative spark to a single sentence. Try it for a post title, a tweet, or even the subject line of your email.

For example,
Your email subject line is: New incentive rules (first draft . . . looks dull).

Other options with creative spark:

- Goodbye existing incentive rules; new rules are welcome.
- Incentives revised: here's how they look now

2. **Touch of persona:** On the 'about' page, you have often read that Ms B. loves gardening, swimming and photography. Reads monotonous, right? It is because the reader is unable to have mental visual images while reading these words. Enable your reader to visualize through the words you use. While choosing to write information about you on your social media profile, be specific and stay away from generic statements.

For example, instead of stating, 'I love travelling,' you could write:

- She calibrated her travel diaries by visiting mesmerizing Switzerland with its high-peaked, snow-capped mountains recently.
- On a weekend, you may find her on one of the weekend getaways with her tent.
- She celebrates her special days with a long drive along the Alps.

The little details make this statement creative.

3. **Metaphors and similes:** Metaphors and similes compare distinct topics and things and appear creative but are very simple to learn. Do you want to try?

Start with the most significant point you want to make in your presentation, where you are presenting a new marketing strategy for your noodle brand, Aggie, targeting college students. Suppose the most important point here is: when you are hungry, prepare tasty Aggie in two minutes.

Experiment with creative ways to make this point. Use different words, metaphors, and similes and observe the differences. You may use:

- Clever Aggie understands your instant hunger.
- Make instant Aggie in the blink of an eye.
- Instant anger is as quick as lightning.

Playing with metaphors and similes is like trying different ingredients to make your final preparation delicious and tempting. It's pretty simple. Write the first draft as it comes to you, and then add some muscle to the words.

Creativity is not just decorative in purpose. In every type of writing for business, you can be creative. Let's take a look at persuasive writing and see how you can be creative even while following the framework of persuasive writing.

Persuasive Writing

Persuasion is the skill of convincing people. Persuasive writing is a genre of writing that requires you to investigate a subject and take a stance on it based on collected and evaluated evidence to convince your reader. It involves making a claim, providing a reason for your claim, and supporting the reason with evidence. In a way, most of the communication you do at the workplace is persuasive in nature, whether it is an idea you are sharing in a meeting, presenting a strategy or a policy, writing an email to a client or manager, negotiating a deal, or writing a report.

The CRE framework makes every communication you do in your professional life easy while adding to your credibility.

'C' stands for claim. A claim is an argument. It is a statement of belief that has the potential to persuade.

For example, we should launch our cracker range in rural areas.

Ensure that your claim is arguable and specific.

'R' stands for reason. A reason is the logical scaffold. It is a logical statement that strengthens your claim.

For example, we should launch our cracker range in rural areas because it is an untapped market with much potential.

The reasoning, logically, supports your claim and makes it tough to be opposed.

Ensure that your reason is logical, related, fair, concrete and rational.

'E' stands for evidence. Evidence is the proof. It is derived from research, field studies and different sources. It proves that the reason you provided supports the claim you made.

For example, we should launch our cracker range in rural areas because it is an untapped market with much potential. Last quarter, TTT Ltd also launched its cashew nut products in rural markets and succeeded.

Ensure that your evidence is relevant, persuasive and specific.

Essence of Persuasion

Aristotle, a Greek philosopher, wrote in 1932 about three ways to use rhetoric and persuasion: logos, pathos and ethos.

Logos: You can persuade by appealing to logic. For this, you may use numbers, data from reliable sources, tangible statistics, reasoning, recorded evidence, etc. Ensure that your appeal to logic matters to your receivers and makes sense to them. Use concrete words and point out the visible benefits to the receiver.

For example, recent studies conclude that HHH sunscreen keeps 80 per cent of sunburn away from you because of its SPF 30, which has been proven in 95 per cent of the subjects on which it was tested.

Pathos: You can persuade by appealing to emotions and feelings. To use pathos, you need to have your audience experience the emotion in order to respond to your persuasion. These emotions may be happiness, fear, flattery, anger, nostalgia and sympathy. Use simple and expressive words and voice modulation (tone in writing). Be subtle while using pathos so that your receiver believes you. Pathos is, generally, very useful in the introduction and conclusion.

For instance, would you like it if, after swimming, you emerged from the pool with sunburn and rashes? I am sure, no. HHH sunscreen shields your skin.

Ethos: You can persuade by appealing to credibility. If you want to persuade people, it is important for them to accept you. People will be persuaded if they trust you. In communication, trust takes time to develop and can be gained in numerous ways. Use suitable words, look honest through your attire and behaviour, excel in what you do, and keep your commitments in order to appeal to credibility. Ethos can be used to persuade through your credibility, a known figure or brand in the field, or a celebrity.

For example, I am Dr Gee, a dermatologist, and I recommend HHH sunscreen to shield your skin.

You may choose to use one of these three appeals based on the context, either in isolation, in pairs, or all three in different proportions together.

After you understand the order of persuasion (CRE) and the types of appeals you can use (logos, pathos and ethos), you should know how attention, interest, desire and action (AIDA) shape persuasion.

The AIDA model of communication is meant to motivate your receiver into action. This can be used in persuasive writing as well as presentations.

AIDA in Business Writing

A for Attention: In the present age of information overload, it is important for you to catch the receiver's attention so that they read or listen to what you have to share. In this part of persuasion, the first few words and the first few moments are very important. Power words and phrases, strong sentences, startling statistics, an example of a brand ambassador, and images are some ways to catch the attention of your receiver. Refrain from pushing your idea or product at this stage; instead, try to pull their attention by using logos, pathos, or ethos individually or in combinations.

I for Interest: After grabbing attention, gradually go on to explain specifically what issue your idea or product is able to solve. The issue you mention at this stage justifies the existence of your idea or product. Make them feel the relevance of your message and focus on its practical value for them. Don't overdo it at this stage; after creating interest, leave your receiver desiring more details.

D for Desire: Now that you have caught their attention and created interest in them, slowly progress to telling them what exactly your idea or product has to offer them. Make use of consideration (your attitude) by sharing the content in simple terms all the time and pointing out what is in it for them. Anticipate questions from the receivers and address them even before they ask you. This proactive communication removes their confusion and doubts. Spend the most of your time in this stage explaining difficult points one by one. CRE facilitates this stage. Here, you need to make a claim, provide reasoning, and support your claim with verifiable evidence. This process will augment your receivers' readiness to take action. Also, back up the desire created by showing how your resolution or proposal is time-bound and how a quick decision from them will benefit them. You can reinforce your statement by sharing other people's testimonies with regard to how your proposition solved their problem and helped them.

A for Action: While still sticking to your attitude, share the action you want the receivers to take for their benefit. Give them the details they need to take action by including a limited-time offer discount, timelines and contact details, including social media handles.

AIDA works better in communication with an indirect approach. While using AIDA in an email or memo, catch the reader's attention with the subject line without divulging details there. The main idea is to be saved for the end. On the other hand, having communication with a direct approach does work if used sensibly, where you catch attention with the main idea, build interest with details, and, by indicating the issue and sharing the resolution, create a desire with evidence; and, finally, close with your expectation for action after reinforcing your main proposition.

AIDA in Presentations

Presentations are quite popular at the workplace to communicate within and outside of organizations. After discussing how AIDA can be used in business writing with creativity, let us see how it can be used to structure your presentations effectively. Every presentation begins with an introduction and closes with a conclusion. Whether you are presenting a novel idea or an ongoing assignment, AIDA can lead to the outcome you desire from your receivers.

Attention: Grab the attention of your audience with your opening remarks and slides. The initial slides should set the stage for your presentation. For example, if you are sharing a new service, show it visually through images or video that carry brief information about its features and the problems it solves.

Interest: After grabbing attention in this manner, feed the interest of your receivers. Provide in-depth information about the idea you talked about and build their interest. This can be done by talking about the advantages your service brings to them, by comparing your service with the existing ones, and by showing how your service has an edge over others. For example, in the case of a new idea, talk about the main features of the service in detail, how it is different from others, and its unique selling proposition.

Desire: Keep it short. You cannot risk losing the attention of your audience at this stage. Make it as exciting as possible. For example, dwell on the timeliness of the service you have proposed and emphasize how it will be redundant if action is delayed. Animation effects and infographics have the potential to enhance your presentation at this stage.

Action: This is the stage where you set your expectations with the receivers with regard to action. Provide additional information with contact details so they may resort to action quickly.

Making AIDA Power-Packed

Make your use of AIDA powerful with the following guidelines:

Use Present Tense: When you write in the present tense, the problem is perceived as relevant. The present tense shows how important the problem is and how quickly you need to act. Past tense makes the issue outdated, and future tense shows the issue is not very important at the moment.

Timely Persuasion: Time your persuasion strategically. Persuasion done in time and responded to promptly gets you success in your intention.

Striking Visuals: The numbers, graphs, images, figures and statistics you use to authenticate your claim as evidence. Stress on vital figures and words to add emphasis.

Emotions and Feelings: Polish your skill at adding a creative spark to your choice of words, especially those catering to the emotions and feelings of your receivers. Add the right phrases, words and pictures to make your persuasion more emotional by touching their core feelings. Refrain from taking it too far.

Convincing: By being convincing, you ascertain that your receiver will respond positively. When you communicate with the intention to convince, it affects the way you write. Your writing, both words and tone, becomes more positive and persuasive.

Trustworthiness: You have already added trust to your writing through facts and figures. Make your persuasion more trustworthy by adding recommendations and endorsements from distinguished individuals with credibility.

In a Nutshell

A creative and persuasive style of business writing and making business presentations provides you with a boost on your way to the pinnacle of success. A proper structure in such efforts (CRE) facilitates understanding and enhances your impression.

8

Social Media Web and the AI Block

Content is fire, social media is gasoline.

—Jay Baer

The Changing Face of Communication in the Era of Artificial Intelligence (AI)

> You: Hey, Siri!
> Siri: Hey, how are you doing?
> You: Hey, Siri. I want to order a pizza. Give some options.

Siri provides a host of options.

At another time, if you ask her to show you a direction, she will show the map on your device and you just press start to move ahead.

Isn't this amusing? Doesn't it appear magical? AI has made all this possible.

The term AI brings to mind machines, chatbots and robots, but AI is not as scary as we might have perceived.

AI has enabled computers to speed up tasks requiring human acumen. Today, our lives largely depend on AI, whether it is the adjustment of room temperature, cooking temperature, or when e-commerce sites give suggestions based on our browsing details. Everything is happening because of AI.

Communication is at the core of human existence. It is the key to all problems, and, therefore, we, as human beings, make every effort to bring comfort and ease to the way we communicate with each other in order to make it more effective. Technology has by far played an important role in evolving the way we communicate. From writing physical letters and sending them through post offices, we entered the age of telephone and fax messages, moving on to electronic communication and cell phones, and we have reached instant messaging and communicating through applications and social media networks, and we are still moving on. Thanks to the AI, IoT, augmented reality, and other technologies that have made this possible. Along with making an entry into every part of our business, these technologies have created a significant place in our lives. These technologies have made communication faster with our close ones as well as with everyone else who is on the web with a connection. Cortana and Siri have become household names now.

AI has completely transformed our workspaces and our organizations. It has specifically revolutionized communication in the workplace. Most advanced tools and applications have made it possible for different divisions of the organization to communicate with digital speed, and that too, efficiently. Communication with internal stakeholders, like horizontal and diagonal communication between inter- and intra-divisions, upward communication from employees to management or supervisors, and downward communication from management or supervisors to employees, as well as communication with external stakeholders like customers, clients, the public, etc., have been made easier and quicker due to AI.

Tools and chatbots have become part of our routine, whether we use them to set alerts, schedule, or plan and execute our projects. AI has made complex processes simple, thereby increasing our productivity and saving us time.

AI and Internal Communication

Businesses have been busy devising new ways to communicate and connect with their customers, clients, the general public, other organizations and government agencies. Internal communication has taken a back seat for a long time. However, with the need to create engagement with the employees, businesses are now exploring various ways to connect with them and engage with them.

Most of the organizations have realized how vital employees are to their success and are doing everything possible to set up relations with them. AI has made internal communication much more feasible, easier and interesting. An organization that is strong within, with its internal stakeholders understanding its essence and existence as well as core values, excels and sustains longer as compared to those that do not value their internal stakeholders and consider them merely capital.

A gift of AI, natural language processing (NLP), has made it feasible for organizations to communicate better. In its present advanced stage, NLP determines syntax and semantics and does sentiment analysis accurately. These features strengthen the organization's bond with its employees by facilitating downward communication, where messages are perceived by the employees as conversations and not orders. This includes all types of communication, whether an expression of appreciation or a routine email message. Bringing all employees onto the same page and with a similar understanding is difficult for businesses in an age where remote working is slowly becoming the 'new normal,' and NLP has the solution.

Instagram, through its feed feature, gives liberty to organizations to share important information and announcements with their employees, and design achievement stories. Chatbots are being used to connect meaningfully with the employees, helping them do a self-SWOT (strengths, weaknesses, opportunities, and threats) analysis and providing input on improvements. At times, people are uncomfortable sharing or asking things, especially the sensitive ones with the managers, and that is where the chatbot comes to the rescue. Making efficient use of AI can work wonders in the field of workplace communication.

Corporate communication is based on trust, which gives an organization's stakeholders confidence in it. The way an organization talks to people is a big part of why people trust and believe in it, and why they will continue to do so. Following are the areas where AI is creating ripples:

Public Speaking: Public speaking is a key element in communication. Somehow, people have believed, since time immemorial, that those with a flair for writing and speaking are not good at math or science, and vice versa. Here's the good news: AI enables you to do what you once felt was impossible. This is through hybrid thinking, which is due to the chemistry created by AI between real and virtual intelligence.

Message Creation and Delivery: Most often, you are anxious about the message you have drafted and whether it will communicate what you intend to and get the expected result. It turns out to be very expensive to talk with the recipients, interview and survey them, and keep an eye on them. AI, on the other hand, has made it possible to simulate a message, and the sender can easily find out how the message will get there and make a guess about what will happen.

Choice of Words: NLP helps you choose the right words to use in your message. This is done through content analysis and text mining techniques. AI gives you a picture of how your message will come across to your audience and how clear and interesting it will be, all based on algorithms. AI enables you to be considerate and follow you-attitude in communication.

Impact of Delivery: AI has made it possible for you to check your paralanguage while you are delivering a message. It can analyse your voice modulation, body language and facial expressions. How fruitful it is when you get to know the receivers' views simultaneously! It enables you to customize your delivery to them. The same technique can be used during meetings with your colleagues, clients, and others communicating with you.

Harnessing AI within Your Organization

1. **Understand the best in your team members:** You are very well aware that money can buy you things, but not the happiness that you derive from job satisfaction. And job satisfaction is possible when

you do the work you are best at and like the most. Discussing the best with each team member is time consuming. Based on simple information collected from your team, AI helps you identify the skills and interests of your team members so that you can keep them engaged and they can enjoy what they are doing.

2. **Declutter the discussions:** Often, groups tend to digress from the main topic, resulting in wastage of time and energy. AI enables you to shut down groups from unproductive chats. It can also check for unsolicited and useless messages.

3. **Gamification:** Gamification is the use of games for activities like rewards, competition, and training at the workplace. When you make a task look like a game and link it to a reward, employees become very motivated and excited. Choose the game in alignment with your objectives, share your plan of action with the employees, set clear goals, and start the game. With this fun way to learn and do work, your employees will be more interested and productive.

4. **AI translator:** We are a part of a global workforce, and language might be the biggest barrier to cross-cultural communication within the organization, and across geographies. English might be the lingua franca, but some words may still cause issues. The AI translator comes in handy in tackling such situations.

5. **Tailored experiences:** Today, each one of us likes tailored experiences, which have been made possible by AI. Similarly, your employees need tailored experiences at their workspaces. Tailor the emails you send to employees; add a personal touch to make them feel special; and encourage them to reply to your emails. Customize your employees' WhatsApp and other instant messages. Even though it is a general message, personalize it by adding their name or something related to their habit or preference.

6. **Have a dialogue:** Proactively use AI to create a dialogue between you and your team. Start an interactive news board or newsletter with ideas from your team. Use chatbots and virtual platforms for your team to showcase their talents. Create an atmosphere of camaraderie within the team instead of pitting them against each other.

Barriers to Digital Communication

Even though AI has made communication easier, there are still problems with digital communication that we need to solve before we can get the most out of email, apps, social media, messages, websites, and other ways of communicating digitally.

1. **Environmental Barriers:** Environmental barriers like time, place, and channel create a hindrance

to digital communication. Time can be a problem if you don't have time to answer your messages during the day, if you don't have time to update your website, or if the time you send a message doesn't match the time the other person is online. A place barrier occurs when you communicate with people on platforms they don't or rarely use. Channel is a barrier if your algorithms cause an issue or due to problems with the connectivity.

Way out: Plan your time to handle daily messages efficiently. Delegate website-updating work to skilled hands. Identify the platforms most used by your target receivers and use those for better listening from them. Have a well-established technology team to keep the software, hardware and connectivity in order.

2. **Psychological Barriers:** Psychological barriers include emotions, perceptions, attitudes and belief systems of people. In digital communication, just sharing the information is not enough if it is not received in the right spirit and acted upon if required. In the absence of non-verbal communication, it becomes difficult for your receiver to interpret your message as you intended.

Way out: Before sending the message across, take a pause and read the draft message with empathy. Anticipate the response you want from the receiver, read your message again, and adjust the tone of your words to get a positive outcome. Remember that your email, tweet, message, or post needs to be read without emotional filters, so your tone and word choice need to be very sensitive and non-discriminatory.

3. **Language and Semantic Barriers:** While hashtags, memes, and emojis are the latest trends in digital communication and very helpful in conveying complicated ideas, they may become barriers if you and your receivers do not share a similar understanding. Language, jargon, and slang also cause barriers in digital communication.

Way out: Use words that have a single meaning and are inclusive in nature. Communicate in a language understood by your receiver. Make use of universally accepted emojis and acronyms. Share the meaning of the hashtags with your recipients before using them. Be sensitive to what different words might mean in different cultures while communicating digitally.

4. **Credibility Barriers:** Credibility barriers result in the absence of trust for the sender, the message and the medium. In the digital age, with AI, even the chances of getting duped have increased manifold. People do fall for fake videos and photoshopped images, so they work with technology companies to protect their accounts and personal data. Still,

there is no sure shot formula their details will be safe. Your emails and messages do come under the scanner if you are not perceived as credible.

Way out: Develop trust and credibility in your receivers by being transparent and by opening a conversation with them rather than just sending messages. Their involvement in the process will augment their trust in you.

Untangling the Social Media Web

The reason behind the success of every team is good communication. Think about how easy it has become to work from home now that we can connect with each other through platforms like Microsoft Teams or Slack. Technology has made it simple to be connected with the team to enhance communication. Social media has done wonders for bolstering internal communication. There are many areas where social media has made communication within the team more efficient, thereby increasing the productivity of the team. When there is frequent open communication among the team members and the leader, the exchange of information is easy, issues are resolved quickly, questions are answered diligently, and a lot of time is saved. Teams get demotivated when they feel left out of decision-making and feel motivated when their opinions are sought and taken seriously. Social media, therefore, becomes an important tool in internal communication. To begin with, social media replaces the monotony of mundane emails and newsletters with exciting and helpful content and makes your employees more cooperative. Social media integration for developing stimulating communication has great potential to make your teams more efficient, engaged and motivated. Some examples are as follows:

Facebook page: If you have a private page on Facebook, you can share news about your business and send regular messages. You can use this page to tell people about meetings, post about deadlines that are coming up, and inspire them. You can post fun games and activities to make it more fun, and your team can take part in different contests.

Blog: Create a knowledge bank by making a blog where your coworkers can talk about different work-related topics. Write the blog in simple language without jargon. A blog is beneficial to your new team members, who may hesitate to ask questions initially, and also to the existing team members, who can strengthen their bond with the team. Competitions and contributions involving the entire organization will make your blog lively. A blog also helps in gaining authentic feedback from colleagues on existing policies, changes planned, mergers, future plans, and much more.

Twitter: By setting your Twitter account to private mode, you can tweet with your colleagues about promotions, retirements, the daily news of your organization, birthdays, and the hidden talents of colleagues. You may customize the tweets and make them theme-based, changing themes every month or every quarter. Themes may include professional development, motivation, team building, well-being, etc. Make these tweets as interactive and fun-filled as possible.

LinkedIn: Organizational LinkedIn groups can be used to add value to employees. A company profile, along with a brief biography of every key employee, proves quite beneficial. This group can be used to post event information, notices, important announcements and meeting details. You can use it as a Facebook private page, with the difference that this platform calls for more formality and professionalism.

LinkedIn also works wonders as your professional network for growth. This is how you can use it richly.

Your LinkedIn Profile Is Your Curriculum Vitae

Update and complete it, as it is visible to other registered LinkedIn users. The visibility of your profile depends on whether you keep it private or public. A public profile enables non-LinkedIn users to also see your profile. When searching on LinkedIn, the search mechanism prioritizes complete profiles, so complete your profile by

- adding your photograph, clicked professionally; there should be warmth on your face in the photograph added;
- inserting a cover image or background image highlighting your profession;
- referring to your organization and location;
- including a brief description of who you are, what you do, and your area of expertise;
- appending your present position and responsibilities;
- including your education details, work experience (if any), and at least three strengths.

Make and keep connections: LinkedIn makes it easy to create social networks, which help you keep up with what's going on in your field(s) of interest and share information. Once you form a connection with another LinkedIn user, you can start interacting with or following the connection. Fortify the formed connections by finding common interests or skills. Refrain from intruding into the personal space of the connection. Begin with the exchange of pleasantries and inquiring about professional issues; develop a bond; and stay connected. Make connections on LinkedIn for professional growth, not just to take advantage of the connection.

Recommendation and endorsement: A recommendation is a personal testimonial showcasing your skills and expertise. Ensure you have at least four to five recommendations on your account. Request your acquaintances, colleagues, clients, and managers to write recommendations for you highlighting your qualities and professionalism in specific terms. An endorsement is confirmation of a specific skill that you possess. It comes as a notification of endorsement. Getting recommendations and endorsements boosts your profile and adds credibility to it.

Groups: Make and join LinkedIn groups and read and share ideas, news, and updates related to the group's topic. This will help you build your network. Once you make a request to join a group and are added to it, you can communicate with and ask questions of other members of the group. Maintain a code of conduct as a group member.

Content writing: Like other social networks, LinkedIn lets you share images, messages, presentations, videos and posts. While sharing posts from other users, ensure your posts are enlightening and pertinent ones. You may create your own posts with interesting insights in an appealing language. Add hashtags to increase the readership of your post or article on LinkedIn. Experiment with different hashtags to enable your post or article to reach more users. LinkedIn connects you with the past, present, and future and is a great way to showcase 'brand you.'

Social Media for Leadership Communication

As a leader, you can get a lot out of social media if you use it to help your organization grow and improve and have a goal in mind. You can improve your company's reputation on social media and build strong relationships with coworkers, management, clients, customers, and suppliers if you plan and act carefully.

Chronicle relevant topics: Whether you are leading a team of three or leading an organization, you can use social media most efficiently by chronicling relevant topics on the social media platforms. If your team handles environment-related projects, you are expected to be an expert in environmental issues. Begin with two to three fundamental topics that are vital to you, your team, and your organization and that you would want to be known for. Consistently post your comments and opinions on these topics on your social networks. This continuous dialogue demonstrates your knowledge and also supports your chronicle.

Crisis management: No organization is immune to crises, but the way the organization handles the crisis makes all the difference. The first important task after a crisis is to acknowledge its occurrence. A quick response to the crisis by sharing how it will be resolved is absolutely necessary. Addressing the issue immediately by first acknowledging that it has happened, taking ownership of the organizational lacunae with an apology, and sharing the potential actions to resolve the problem are the first steps in crisis management. Time is a crucial factor, and the role of social media platforms becomes significant to handle a crisis quickly. A video or an apology has the power to simplify the most complex of issues.

Be in touch: Keeping internal and external stakeholders informed about your company through social networks is part of staying in touch. As a leader or manager, you need not post minute details that will be handled by the team handling your company's social networks. However, in your profile, you should announce major news and focus on company achievements. Your personal intervention in these matters personalizes the social media platforms, fostering trust and credibility for your organization.

Socially aware: Positioning your company as socially aware makes it unique. The need of the hour is to lead to positive changes in society. Ensure that your support for a social cause is sincere and leads to action.

Dealing with Incoming Communication on Social Media

If you decide to use social media, you will get messages that you will have to deal with. Here's how you can do this:

Queries: In case there is a query on your social network, respond to it within 48 hours. It may be a query, an issue, or a complaint. It gives your customer the feeling of being attended to. Others who visit your page also observe your involvement and appreciate your activity.

Negative reviews: Don't panic if you see negative reviews on your page. Try to respond assertively without getting defensive. Address the reason for the negative review and resolve it. Your thoughtful response will enable visitors to understand your perspective. Don't be impolite at any cost.

Positive reviews: Make sure you thank everyone who leaves a positive review or thanks you on your page. People feel nice thinking their reviews have been read.

Check-ins: If a customer posts a check-in at your business or a photo of one of your products or your store, you can show them you appreciate it by liking their posts.

Using Hashtags Right!

A hashtag is a keyword phrase, without spaces, with a pound sign (#) before it. For example, #Ilovemyhome, #SaveWater, and #ToffeeFans are hashtags. Hashtags may be positioned at the start, middle, or end of your posts on social media. They help people search for updates on social media and drive more traffic to your social media handles, especially Instagram and Twitter. They expand your network by making your content visible to more people than just your followers.

In order to make the best use of hashtags, you must know how to use them in a creative way. Here are some basics for using hashtags effectively:

Simplicity: Hashtags that really work are simple and easy to remember. A lengthy hashtag or one with a complex spelling keeps traffic away. Moreover, under the name of creativity, don't use hashtags that people have never wondered about or are searching for. Simplicity combined with familiarity is the key to attracting more people. For example, #Ilovemywork

Relevance: Hashtags that are relevant and give specific, short information about the topic are thought to be better. Your skill lies in identifying the likes and interests of your receivers. After identifying these, you can use hashtags to engage with communities. For example, #savetheelephant

Trending hashtags: Trending hashtags are those that have already gained widespread recognition. These are the most discussed hashtags, or those dealing with the current scenario, like #pandemic and #Covid19. Trending hashtags related to your kind of business or relevant to the work you do allow you to reach a wider audience.

Multiple platforms: Hashtags give your brand more personal and professional exposure. So, use them on all the social media platforms for people to retain them for a longer time. Use no more than two hashtags per post on Twitter, Facebook and LinkedIn, while you can go up to ten in the case of Instagram. Overusing hashtags leads to a decline in audience interest and engagement in your posts.

Emojis Etiquette

In Emails

Emojis are used to express emotions digitally. They are symbols used to convey a reaction in emails and text messages to those who can't see your non-verbal behaviour. In other words, emojis are used to convey non-verbal messages in written communication. Emojis are informal and, therefore, should be used thoughtfully in business emails, for these emails demand formality and email etiquette. You may, however, use emojis in informal emails, even at the workplace. Emojis may also be employed when you are writing formal emails to existing clients, customers, or team members, or in marketing or branding emails. These have the advantage of giving a personal touch and adding credibility if used in the proper context and with the proper intent.

In Marketing Emails

You may use emojis in marketing and promotional emails, especially if your potential customers are millennials and Generation Z. While writing promotional emails, emojis work well in the subject line as well as the body of the message since the objective of such emails is based on AIDA. Emojis in the subject lines of such emails draw the recipient's attention and pique their interest in opening and reading the message. Just make sure you are using the emojis that have the same meaning everywhere. Refrain from adding unnecessary and redundant emojis.

In Formal Emails

As time has gone on, the difference between formal and casual emails has become blurred. Emojis have always been fine in casual emails, and they are slowly making their way into formal emails as well. Emojis do add a nonverbal element to messages in formal emails, as long as you follow these rules:

- Learn by observation. If you receive an email with an emoji, it is safer for you to respond to that person using an emoji.
- Don't rush into using an emoji in your first email related to work. You may try once you develop a rapport with the receiver. Even then, try to use it meaningfully and not just for fun.
- Make sure the emojis you use have universal interpretations. Explore the meaning of an emoji while communicating across cultures.
- Be smart when using emojis in internal, formal emails so that they don't cause problems because they are misunderstood.
- Be sensitive to your organizational culture before deciding on using emojis in formal emails.
- Avoid using emojis while dealing with serious issues or complaints.

In a Nutshell

The AI world and social media are tools that you can use to be at the forefront. The only thing to keep in mind is the judicious application of these tools. Alexa and Siri have made life simple, while emojis and memes have made it engaging. With AI in your toolkit and social media as your weapon, you are all set to win the battle of competition.

9

The Four Mantras

Anything's possible if you've got enough nerve.
—J.K. Rowling

Mantra 1: I have a child within (objectivity).

When asked, 'Do you have a child within you?' Most of us would be tempted to say, 'Yes!' If asked, 'Why is it required to have a child within?' The answers will range across an array of words such as energy, joy, curiosity, learning, no tension, happy and eager.

Let's visit our childhood.

When we made the first friend of our lives, did we think of the friend's gender, social status, economic status, or colour? No, we didn't.

When someone complimented us, you could see how pure our happiness was when we said, 'Thank you.'

How long did we go without speaking to a friend after we had a fight? Twenty minutes, one hour, two hours or a day? On the low side, twenty minutes; on the high side, perhaps two hours.

What happened when we grew up? The process of growing up is not bad, but during the process, first due to the influence of our own family, neighbourhood, school and higher education, a lens has developed in front of our eyes. Now, we look at the world and people around us through the lens. We have our own prejudices, biases and presumptions.

People choose their friends based on their preferences, likes and dislikes, among other things. When someone compliments us, we still say, 'Thank you,' but inside our heads pops a question: 'Why?' or 'Does she expect a favour from me?' or 'Is she pulling my leg?' When we have a fight with someone, we stop interacting with the person for days, sometimes weeks or months, and sometimes we just snap all ties.

How happy were we as kids when we took compliments with genuine joy and didn't have any prejudices, biases, or preconceived ideas? When we didn't judge or have opinions? We lived in the moment without judging or making assumptions.

So when you say this first mantra, 'I have a child within' daily, you are promising yourself to be childlike and not childish, throughout the day.

For example, you worked with B on the XYZ project. All through the project, you did most of the work, while B either did not contribute or, whenever she did, did so half-heartedly. The project report was submitted on time, and the work was praised. After a couple of weeks, your manager has a conversation with you as follows:

Manager: You did a wonderful job on the XYZ project. Please do the EFG project too. Will you team up with B?

You are tempted to say one of the following:

If you are close to the manager, you might want to say, 'No way, she does nothing. Please include someone else.'

But if your equation is not that close, you might say, 'May I team up with P on this project?'

That's precisely the moment when you need to apply mantra 1. Remind yourself to be childlike and reply to your manager, 'Sure, I will team up with B again.' However, in order not to be childish, have an open conversation with B before the project starts, set individual goals and tasks, exchange interim progress reports, and develop a bond with B so that, in case of issues, you both might discuss and sort out rather than sulk.

Mantra 2: I love myself (self-acceptance, empathy, assertiveness).

Do you love yourself? OK, OK, wait! What does it mean to 'love oneself'? Here, it implies accepting oneself as one is, with one's strengths and areas for improvement. Yes, you read it right! Do away with the habit of using the word 'weakness'. The moment you call something your 'weakness', you indicate that you are on a dead end and that you are aware of your shortcomings and are happily living with them. On the contrary, when you call your shortcomings 'areas of improvement', you signal to the receiver that you have identified your shortcomings and are trying to work on them.

How does it help? It does in various ways. First and foremost, when you love yourself, you are able to love others. You accept yourself as you are. You do get angry and frustrated, but you don't dwell there forever. You come out of those feelings. When you accept yourself, you are able to accept others. Subconsciously, you learn empathy, which is an important element of communication. Your choice of words and tone reflect your empathy. You deliberately choose to use specific words and tone to add effect to what you say.

Second, if you love yourself, you have enhanced self-esteem, and you are able to stand up for yourself and take a stance. It makes you assertive in your behaviour. People around you trust you in times of trouble and know that you will help them, but they are also aware that you won't do it at your expense. You won't need to put this into words. The way you treat people is enough to demonstrate your assertiveness.

Third, if you love yourself, others will love you. This simply means that people will think twice about taking advantage of you because your self-esteem, empathy and assertiveness have demonstrated your self-acceptance.

Mantra 3: I will never ever close the doors of communication (assertiveness).

In a forest named Jungle, there lived a bear who was the king of the forest. He was the largest in that jungle, so he became the king. One day, the bear decided to eat other animals and, accordingly, issued a circular and got it circulated. It read, 'I am going to eat one animal every day.' The cycle of one animal going to the bear's den every day to be eaten begins. Some animals somehow manage to escape, while most of them are eaten up by the bear. Three animals are left in the jungle now, in addition to the bear. The bear allowed every animal to ask two questions before eating it.

The animal known for cleverness, a fox, enters the bear's den trembling and crying.

Fox: Is it true you have a list of animals you want to eat?

Bear: Yes.

Fox: Am I there on the list?

Bear: Yes.

The fox gets eaten up.

The next day, a wolf enters the bear's den, trembling and crying.

Wolf: Is it true you have a list of animals you want to eat?

Bear: Yes.

Wolf: Am I there on the list?

Bear: Yes.

The wolf gets eaten up.

The next day, a rabbit enters the bear's den, dancing, singing and laughing.

Rabbit: Am I there on your list?

Bear: Yes.

Rabbit: Can you remove me from there?

Bear: Uh, yes.

So, here it is!

The rabbit chose to ask the right questions, and since the bear said yes to both questions, it worked. Moreover, the first two animals asked a redundant question, 'Is it true you have a list of animals you want to eat?' It was a circular. Imagine a manager issuing a circular and, 10 minutes later, a team member asking her whether it was issued by her. Also, the rabbit chose to ask to be removed. Whether it is a request you want to make to your colleague or your manager, how often have you wondered what if it's a 'No'? Say to yourself, 'I will never ever close the doors of communication. I will keep them open, always.'

Mantra 4: I will never react; I will always respond (authenticity).

What happens when you receive a nasty email full of flaming from a team member with false allegations and blame? Don't you click the reply button, type a nastier, even more powerful reply, hit the send button and feel relieved? Most of us, many a time, do this. This is referred to as a reaction. A suggestion here is to type all that comes to mind in the reply box but save it as a draft before hitting the send button. Divert your mind to some other work and return to the draft after some time. You will find yourself either cutting the flab by 10 percent, smiling at what you have written, or deleting the draft altogether and rewriting the reply. This is called a response.

While reactions may be impulsive, aggressive and emotional, responses are mostly cautious, mild and thoughtful. Choose to respond. Don't think that responses take forever. It is a myth. Even responses can be quick. What differentiates a reaction from a response is a pause. A pause gives both you and the receiver time to take charge of their emotions and think before saying or writing anything. A pause may be for a few seconds where you divert your mind into something else, even if it is a change of screen, looking into a report, or just sitting still and understanding your present state of mind, identifying your emotions.

These four pillars go a long way towards shaping our communication, right from the choice of words to the tone and delivery. These help fulfil the long-term goal of communication—maintaining relationships.

How Is Self-Esteem Important in Communication?

Self-esteem is the image you have of yourself. How you feel and behave towards yourself plays a significant role in your existence. Self-esteem plays a key role in the way you communicate. Low self-esteem results in low confidence, which directly impacts your communication. You lose confidence in expressing your emotions and thoughts. High self-esteem, on the other hand, boosts your morale and facilitates effective communication.

Developing self-esteem is a gradual process that you need to nurture like a plant. It does not grow on its own, nor does it grow overnight. The way you feel about yourself and the way you treat yourself have an effect on your self-esteem.

For example, you meet your team on four consecutive days and say, 'I am a loser. Whatever I do does not succeed. I have given up.' On the fifth day, one of your team members will start using the same words for you. This is what happens when, due to low self-esteem, you demean yourself, people around you start doing the same. While being aware of your shortcomings and working on their improvement, it is very much required of you to find pride in your achievements, big or small, significant or not. You need not be arrogant or boastful about them; however, a healthy pride in your achievements leads you to walk with your head held high and your voice full of energy.

Self-esteem leads you to become emotionally strong with a high emotional quotient, which ultimately leads you to value people in your life and around you. Your self-esteem makes you trust your work and leads you to empathy, where you unknowingly start behaving with people around you as you want them to behave with you. You will stop blaming people if something goes wrong or if they are at fault. On the other hand, once you've had your first setback, you'll be more interested in how to fix things than in what went wrong. That gives birth to 'never say die' attitude in your life. With a high sense of self-worth, you gain the power to manage and shape adverse situations and set things right through powerful communication.

You are the only person who can help you build self-esteem. No outside situation or person can do this for you unless you ask them to. Self-esteem deteriorates due to many reasons, such as perceived injustice, bad performance, negative thoughts, and a distorted image of yourself. External circumstances may harm your self-esteem, but no external motivator can help revive it until you decide to let it happen. Communication, as you know, is not limited to words. Your body and your tone also get affected along with the words owing to low self-esteem. Low self-esteem affects your choice of words and tone, which become passive or aggressive, pushing you away from assertiveness. The effect of passive and aggressive communication is that you lose your peace of mind, which eventually affects your physical and mental well-being.

How Is Self-Confidence Important in Communication?

High self-esteem leads to self-confidence. Self-confidence is the quality of believing in yourself, irrespective of your areas of improvement or what others might think about you. When you are confident, you control your life and do not permit external influences to destroy it. You develop the ability to see a ray of hope at the end of every dark tunnel. Your self-confidence fills you with positivity and optimism and is visible to everyone through the way you appear, communicate and behave.

Self-confidence makes you bold to seek clarifications while communicating, making you disciplined and punctual at the same time. You are able to articulate with clarity of thought, which leads to less misunderstanding in communication. Because you have an open mind, you can listen carefully, respect different points of view, and say what you want to say succinctly. Your self-confidence empowers you to learn from your and others' mistakes, correct yourself when you are criticized, and stops you from accusing people and circumstances for your faults. You own up to your mistakes and try to correct them.

Your self-confidence encourages you to take calculated risks and put in extra efforts to reach your targets. People with self-confidence accept compliments with grace: 'Thank you for the appreciation. I certainly put in a lot of effort on that project.' Your self-confidence makes you an ideal leader and a good team player because you participate without being egoistic and on the merits of the situation.

Action Plan to Enhance Your Self-Confidence

You can boost your confidence by getting better at what you do and becoming more positive about yourself. Here are some ways you can achieve this:

1. **Improve your appearance:** Self-grooming can do wonders for your self-confidence. A nice shower followed by wearing a good outfit makes you feel great about yourself. It adds to your self-confidence.
2. **Positive thoughts in, negative thoughts out:** Replace your negative thoughts with positive ones. It appears difficult, but regular exercise makes it possible. When the thought, 'I can't do it,' occurs to you, don't crouch under it helplessly; just fight it with another one: 'I can do it.' Your talk with yourself is very crucial. While conversing with yourself, deliberately remove the negative words and thoughts and fill the space with positive ones. Destroy your negative thoughts. Remember, only you can do it. Also, complement your positive thoughts with positive action. If your positive

thought is, 'I can do it,' then follow it up by actually doing it. Positive thoughts and actions will lead you to positive discussions with people, and your approach to communication and interpersonal behaviour will become more constructive.

3. **Adjust your speaking speed:** An intelligent and humble person always speaks at a slow pace. It signifies confidence. Your self-confidence helps you understand the importance of adjusting your speaking speed according to your audience.

4. **Posture:** Posture indicates your level of self-confidence. When you stand tall, you have a great feeling about yourself. It communicates your demeanour to the receiver even before you start interacting.

5. **Be competent and prepared:** There is no better strategy for being confident than being competent and prepared. When you have the needed skills and are prepared, it affects your self-confidence positively and shows through your gestures, eye contact and words. Keep yourself updated, and you will gain the power of thinking on your feet and sharing opinions about the surroundings during a conversation.

6. **Don't be a whiner:** Problems never bother you if you seek solutions, and the moment you become a solution-seeker, you get to be known as a go-getter. Your enthusiasm becomes contagious for people around you, and you become an inspiration.

7. **Smile:** Yes, you read it right! A smile costs you nothing but adds to your face value. The moment you smile, you feel better, and the moment you feel better, it affects your tone, and your tone works wonders while communicating. It also adds warmth to your personality, and you are perceived as a cheerful individual.

8. **Cut the clutter:** A clean workstation impacts your productivity and sends a message of your sincerity and diligence even without your saying it. A cluttered workspace often keeps you confused and irritated. Pacify the hurricane within you by cutting the clutter from your workspace.

9. **Get closer to yourself:** It helps. A battle cannot be won without understanding your adversary. When you are trying to work on your self-confidence, you need to first get closer to yourself. Be aware of your thoughts, identify your states of mind, and listen to your feelings and thoughts. If you harbour negative thoughts, acknowledge and evaluate them to get over them. Recognize what needs to be changed within you and work on changing it. These actions will gradually enhance your self-confidence, leading you to become better at communication.

10. **Physical and mental well-being:** A healthy body goes a long way toward increasing your self-confidence.

Workout to develop and maintain it. A healthy mind accomplishes similar tasks. Exercise and strengthen your mental well-being by having and expressing gratitude to others and by appreciating them. It adds to your personal likeability index.

Assertive Behaviour

The foundation of assertiveness is reciprocal in nature. Therefore, being assertive results in tactful communication. In simple words, being assertive means to stand up for yourself and, at the same time, not harm others' interests. It asserts your rights while also being mindful of others' rights. Being assertive is better than being a passive, aggressive, or passive-aggressive communicator. All three of them cause the receiver to react, while assertive behaviour leads to a response.

Passive Behaviour

Passive behaviour, as the name indicates, is to be passive in behaviour, saying yes to everything, avoiding conflict, and letting others take advantage of your passivity. Passive people just accept doing whatever their team decides. They do this to avoid conflict and confrontations, but their doing so makes others feel their feelings are not important at all.

Let's take an example. Your colleague leaves the office early to attend to her guests, and she asks you to finish the last part of her presentation and submit it on her behalf. You say yes despite your own project timeline the same evening. The additional responsibility means working more hours and missing an outing with your family. You were just being nice when you said yes, but in the process, you could not maintain the work-life balance. Such behaviour might stress you and fill you with bitterness and anger, which, in turn, would snatch your peace of mind.

Aggressive Behaviour

Aggressive behaviour, again as per its name, is to be aggressive in whatever you do and say. Aggressive people have no respect for others' needs and feelings. They consider themselves superior and find no harm in embarrassing and bullying others. Aggressive people might get what they want by force, but in the process, they lose their respect. They always judge, condemn and disagree with others. People start avoiding them.

For example, your colleague requests that you tell her how to close a letter to an important client while you are leaving office. You wave your hand, saying, 'Now? No way. Can't you see I am leaving?' Your aggressive behaviour strains your relationship with your colleague.

Passive–Aggressive Behaviour

A combination of passive and aggressive behaviours is called passive-aggressive behaviour. This behaviour makes one behave aggressively in a passive manner. These people don't shout or intimidate others with force like the aggressive people, but instead express their aggression passively, using sarcasm or talking behind their backs. Their resentment is seen through their unhealthy behaviour and negative outlook towards everything and everyone. They are seen as cynics.

For instance, you went to a meeting that the HR department of your company organized to talk about the brand-new performance-based incentive plan. She opened the forum for questions after discussing the policy. You had some queries, but you chose to keep quiet at that time and started discussing the queries sarcastically with other colleagues after the meeting. This behaviour makes you lose credibility at the workplace.

Why Assertive Communication?

- Benefits both you and the receiver.
- Prevents others from taking advantage of you.
- Fosters healthy workplace relationships.
- Helps you to give and gain respect.
- Enhances self-esteem.
- Keeps away stress.
- Gains trust.

How Can I Become Better at Assertive Communication?

Follow the following strategies to become better at assertive communication.

1. **Facts, facts, facts:** Whenever discussing a change in someone's behaviour, just use facts and don't judge the person. For example, your colleague always forgets to complete the task assigned to him. On one such occasion, you might want to say, 'Again, you forgot! You always forget to complete the task assigned to you.' This is unsuitable. Instead, say assertively, 'We were supposed to submit the project today, but you are still to complete the task assigned to you.'

Such a statement shows your openness to your colleague, who might have a valid reason for not completing the task at hand. Don't be quick to assume he did it because he always does so. There is a small line between sounding aggressive and assertive, and that is because of your body language and tone. Stand tall with proper eye contact and speak firmly in a relaxed manner.

2. **'I' messages:** Sentences that begin with 'you' in a conversation frequently come across as judgemental and make your receiver defensive. On the other hand, sentences beginning with 'I' express your feelings and show how others' behaviour has affected you. These 'I' statements empower you to own your reactions and not blame others, thus making even the most conflicting situation appear normal. For example, instead of saying, 'You need to look at the offer and accept it,' try saying, 'I

would like it if you looked at the offer and accepted it.' Instead of saying, 'You're mistaken,' say, 'I disagree.'

3. **Learn to Say 'No':** Make it a habit to say 'no.' In order to communicate assertively, you will have to forego the feeling that you are born to keep everyone around you happy, even at your own cost, and behave the way they dictate. You need to understand that it is absolutely fine to say what you wish, as long as you are not hurting anyone's interests. The best way to do this is to use 'because'. As long as you are providing a reason for saying 'no', you are being assertive. A negative response becomes acceptable when you provide valid reasons with firmness of tone. Providing an option after saying 'no' also helps.

4. **Watch out for your non-verbal communication:** Have proper control over your body language, tone and eye contact. Let all of these be assertive. Maintaining a healthy eye contact adds to the credibility of your words. Have open body language and a neutral expression on your face. Speak in a calm voice. Don't get provoked and lose control of the tranquility of your voice. The right tone and pitch make you sound assertive.

5. **Don't be controlled by emotions:** This is quite challenging, especially when you are angry, extremely sad, or agitated. Acknowledge your emotions and choose to discuss them at another

time when you have controlled them. In case time does not permit you to control your emotions, take a deep breath, tell yourself, 'I will be assertive,' and go ahead.

6. **Mind the verbs:** Choose specific and clear verbs to appear neither flattering nor angry. Use verbs such as will, choose to, want, etc. Avoid verbs like should, could, need, must, have to, etc.

7. **Be in the moment:** Be in the moment while communicating so that your past experience with the same person might not colour your present communication and you don't end up being either aggressive or passive with the person. Mindfulness helps you live in the moment and communicate assertively.

Mindfulness

Mindfulness can be defined as 'focusing in a specific manner on aim, awareness and approval.' This includes the aim of living with an awareness of the present for its approval. Mindfulness, in its simplest form, is living in the moment. It has numerous health advantages like stress relief, better sleep, improved immunity and serenity within. Mindfulness trains you to accept life with an open mind. It boosts your emotional well-being, which, in turn, affects your personal and professional lives positively, further impacting your communication.

Aim, Awareness, Approval

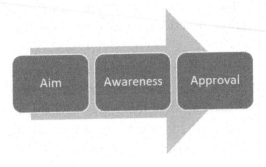

What's Wrong with Our Listening?

The problem with our listening is that most of the time we are engaged in non-listening behaviours (refer to Chapter 2). As a result, we multitask—watching news on television while cutting vegetables, receiving phone calls while answering emails, discussing home issues with our spouses while watering the plants. Many times, we are listening without being in the moment. Mindful listening is when you are able to experience and relate to the speaker.

Follow some simple steps to become a mindful listener.

1. **Concentrate:** Cut all the surrounding sounds and concentrate on the speaker. Silence your phone for all calls and notifications, and switch on the speaker alone. Don't wander into the past or think about the future while listening. The same way

you deliberately bring yourself back when your mind starts wandering during contemplation or meditation, practice the same while focusing on the speaker.

2. **Don't speak.** While listening, just listen. Don't be tempted to speak, even if you have something to offer. Wait until the speaker has finished, and speak when it is time for you to share your thoughts and suggestions. This requires endurance but is not impossible.

3. **Acknowledge:** While listening, it is not required of you to accept or confirm what you are listening, just an acknowledgement is expected, which indicates that you allow the speaker to express. Acknowledgement happens through warmth in your body language and neutral facial expressions.

Mindful listening makes it possible to connect, which is a requirement for mindful communication, and these steps will make sure that you are listening mindfully.

Why Mindful Communication?

Mindful communication can make a big difference in your life and is important because:

- It helps you be objective.
- It helps you to listen.

- Creates a healthy environment for your family, friends and colleagues at work.
- Makes you value people and their opinions.
- Facilitates your taking charge of your life.

Simple Techniques for Developing Mindfulness

When you read the word 'mindfulness', complex ways of meditating and time-consuming exercises come to mind. Don't worry! The following techniques will change your notion altogether.

Technique 1: Mind Your Breath

This technique is fine for a few seconds, a few minutes, or longer than that. It can be done anywhere—just before an interview, a critical meeting, or a potential confrontation.

- Sit straight in a chair or on the ground. Your hands are to be on your lap. You may choose to close your eyes or keep them open, looking down. Now, concentrate on your nostrils and stomach as you inhale and exhale during breathing.
- There is no need to alter your breathing pattern. Count your breaths. Count one after each cycle of breathing in and breathing out. Count until ten cycles remain.

- You might get distracted while counting after every cycle. It's fine and natural. Bring yourself tenderly back to counting whenever you feel distracted.
- After the count of ten, stop counting and just concentrate on your inhaling and exhaling processes. Shepherd your mind back to inhaling and exhaling in case of distractions. This process of focusing with deliberate effort is called mindfulness.
- Don't feel guilty if you start daydreaming or if your mind strolls around. Simply acknowledge the distraction and return to what you were doing.

Technique 2: Develop Mindful Habits

We are all very busy, physically as well as mentally. While physically working on the laptop, your mind is calculating the time left before the next meeting and you are waiting for a message you are expecting. In your busy schedule, don't forget mindfulness, develop mindful habits and make sure you don't miss them. Weave these simple habits into your daily schedule. These may be self-help motivational readings, retiring to bed a little early, and pampering yourself.

Technique 3: Digital Detox

We are, most of the time, digitally connected, either watching, listening or communicating on media.

At times, we feel addicted to the digital world. This addiction leads to mental stress and makes us live either in the past or in the future. Excessive use of digital devices leads to physiological and mental issues, further affecting your communication and behaviour. Attempt a digital detox as a mindfulness exercise. You may not give away your digital devices altogether. However, you may consider a digital fast for either some hours every day or a day or two in a week. You may also choose to limit the use of social media sites during some part of the day or while having food. Another option might be to have a particular detox, like from some apps or games.

Digital detox facilitates living in the moment and focusing on the person you are interacting with rather than looking for messages on your phone or eyeing the laptop screen simultaneously.

Technique 4: Visualization through Guided Imagery

Guided imagery is a simple technique that helps you to de-stress and relax simultaneously. It is as effortless as slipping into a lively daydream and can be done anywhere. It brings you closer to your insights and wisdom and helps you become more resilient and mindful. Guided imagery can be practised without much expense or investment of time. You may either take a class guided by an instructor, use freely available audio recordings, record your own guided imagery, or follow your inner voice.

Following is one example that you may record:

I am visiting the Eden Garden today. It is six o'clock in the morning. I am ready in my red casual T-shirt and dark blue jeans. I'm walking out my bedroom door, across the living room, and towards the parking lot. My black sedan is awaiting me. I open the front door of my car, sit in the driving seat, fix my seat belt, and move out of my white, huge main gate. I take the right turn towards the outskirts of the city. Crossing a small bridge over a little lake with blue water, I reach the entrance of the Eden Garden. I park my car outside the gate, near the sign that says, 'Please park your vehicle here,' and enter the large green main gate.

A gush of wind touches my face, and I feel cheerful. As I walk toward the centre of the garden to the fountain, I cross white lily beds on my right and red roses on my left. I also cross a hillock where I see elderly couples doing yoga and practising laughter therapy. I wave at one of the couples, and the couple reciprocates. I reach the fountain and sit by its side. Tiny, colourless water droplets are flying at me with the wind. I am soaked in joy. I feel the bliss of every droplet on my palms, my face and my feet.

After getting the most joyful experience, I realize it is already 7 a.m. I spent an hour with nature. I am on my way back to the green main gate of the garden. I cross the hillock, the white lily beds and the red roses. I move out of the main gate, open my car door, sit in the driving seat, and return home again over the small bridge on the little lake. I drive into my white main gate, park my car, and enter my home whistling.

You may use your imagination to add as many colours as possible to the detailed description and make it as vibrant as possible. The minute details make you sensitive enough to acknowledge the present and live in it. You will observe that you are becoming more mindful.

You may choose to use visualization in yet another way. Visualization is imagining your objective achieved in your mind and then consciously working on getting it. Visualization employs the energy of your subconscious mind. When you are going to attend a conflict resolution meeting, visualize the conflict being resolved, affirm it by saying, 'It will be resolved,' and see what happens. Visualize the way you want to resolve the conflict, and after the visualization exercise, when you are actually attending the meeting, you will find yourself making every attempt to resolve it.

Technique 5: Light the Inside with the Light Outside

This is another simple exercise that you can do to develop your mindfulness. You don't need anyone else to facilitate it.

Look at any source of light around you. The sun, which is a natural source of light, can serve this purpose during the day, and a tube light can do the same during the evening or night. After looking at the source for five seconds, close your eyes while sitting in a relaxed posture with your back straight but relaxed. Don't rest your back against anything. Place your hands on your lap. Making deliberate efforts, feel the light entering you through your forehead, moving to your left eye, and then to your right. Your eyes are enlightened now; they will choose to see only what is good and ignore all that is bad. The light then moves to your nose, then your ears—first the right ear and then the left ear—and enters your mouth, touching your teeth and tongue. Your nose will smell only good things and stay away from the foul ones; your ears will hear only good things and refrain from listening to the bad; and your mouth will eat and speak only good things and stay away from the bad. The light moves to your arms through your shoulders, first to the right arm, then to the left. Your hands have become empowered now. You will try to use them for good and stop them from doing bad. The light now moves to your legs through your thighs. Your legs are stronger now; they will take you to good places and keep you from going to the bad ones.

Initially, when you start adopting any of these techniques, you might try to do it when you are alone. However, once you become an expert and the technique becomes a habit, mindfulness becomes a cake walk. Even while you are surrounded by people, you will be able to adopt the technique in your inner mind and experience the calm it brings.

Technique 6: Take Mindful Breaks

When you get home from work, do you find it difficult to recall what else you could have accomplished? Where did the time fly? These questions increase your fatigue and mental strain. Instead of thinking about these questions in the evening, take frequent, mindful breaks. Break your entire workday into smaller, more realistic milestones. Sit comfortably with your eyes closed, stretch your hands and legs, and congratulate yourself on each accomplishment. If possible, leave your seat, inhale some fresh air, sip a little water and resume work. These short breaks rejuvenate you to handle anything the day has to offer you.

Mindfulness before a Presentation

You have been asked to present the project report. You get shivers just thinking about standing in front of your colleagues. That's where mindfulness comes to your rescue. Right from the preparation of the presentation to its delivery, mindfulness becomes the key.

While planning the presentation, focus on the project report and make efforts to create the presentation without concentrating on anything else. When you are about to give a presentation, get rid of your nerves and replace them with energy by being aware of your surroundings and quickly going over the presentation's main points in your mind. Instead of pacing the room in nervousness, use your movements fruitfully to energize yourself. Use any of the techniques shared previously and get going, and you will see the difference!

Before Sending an Email

After writing every email, save it as a draft and take a pause. Use one of the techniques of mindfulness. After the exercise, read the saved draft with empathy. If the email reads neutral or positive, hit the send button. If not, modify.

While Complimenting Someone

Be concrete while complimenting someone. Be mindful of the words you choose to appreciate. Instead of generic compliments like 'wonderful job!' use the specifics and say, 'I really liked the way you worked on the XYZ project. Every design that you made and every presentation that you made show your sincerity. Awesome! Keep it up!'

Now you see the benefits of mindfulness? With very little effort and time, you gain magnanimously!

In a Nutshell

These four mantras are a panacea for your well-being!
Remember, a healthy mind resides in a healthy body,
and these two lead you to be a contented individual.
Following a regime actually paves your way to a
clutter-free life!

Acknowledgements

Gratitude is a nine-letter word with countless feelings and emotions involved in it!

This book is an upshot of incessant inspiration from Professor Debashis Chatterjee, whether it came through his words or behaviour or personality. His nudge throughout the project is highly appreciated! Interactions with him during the course of this journey have been immensely fruitful. His motivation kept me moving steadily to the goal with persistence, sincerity and diligence.

IIMK faculty colleagues, students and alumni have played a crucial role in bolstering my confidence. Be it brainstorming sessions during meetings with faculty or class discussions with students or notes of appreciation from some of the alumni thanking me for the learnings they drew from my course stating their practical implications. I cannot thank the IIMK family enough! All my faculty colleagues, students and alumni have enriched my efforts in one way or the other.

The relentless support provided by Penguin editors throughout the project has been immense. The inputs from the editing team have added value to the project and were instrumental in facilitating me to add finesse to the project. I thank Theja for the creative illustrations done with extreme precision.

The cheer, inspiration and care received from my family gave me the fuel to work on this project, and I am indebted to them!

Bibliography

Aristotle, *Rhetoric*, 1932, in Cooper, L. (ed.), *The Rhetoric of Aristotle*, Appleton-Century-Crofts.

Corchia, L., *La Logica Dei Processi Culturali: Jurgen Habermas Tra Filosofia e Sociologia* (Logic of Cultural Processes: Jurgen Habermas between Philosophy and Sociology), ECIG, 2010.

Duarte, N., *Resonate: Present Virtual Stories That Transform Audiences,* Wiley Publishers, 2010.

Giddens, A., *Sociology* (4th ed.), Polity Press, 2005.

Griswold, W., *Cultures and Societies in a Changing World*, Pine Forge Press, 2004.

Hall, E.T., *The Silent Language*, Doubleday, 1959.

Hofstede, G., https://geerthofstede.com/culture- geert-hofstede-gert-jan-hofstede/6d-model-of-nationalculture/

Lakey, B., Tardiff, T.A., and Drew, J.B., 'Negative Social Interactions: Assessment and Relations to Social Support, Cognition, and Psychological Distress, *Journal of Social and Clinical Psychology*, 13, 1994, pp. 42–62.

Lawley, E., 'The Sociology of Culture in Computermediated Communication: An Initial Exploration', Seminar in Research Design, 1994, http://aom.jku.at/archiv/ cmc/text/ lawlen01.htm

Shackelford, T.K., 'Self-Esteem in Marriage', *Personality and Individual Differences*, 30 (3), 2001, pp. 371–90.

Swartz, D., *Culture and Power: The Sociology of Pierre Bourdieu*, University of Chicago Press, 1997.

Swidler, A., 'Culture in Action: Symbols and Strategies', *American Sociological Review*, 52 (2), 1986, pp. 273–86.